Advance Praise

"8 *Keys to Safe Trauma Recovery Workbook* is packed with valuable information and practical skills for traumatized individuals! A wonderful new resource for trauma survivors working on their own healing or for therapists and clients working together."

—**Janina Fisher**, author of *Transforming the Living Legacy of Trauma*
and *Healing the Fragmented Selves of Trauma Survivors*

"Supplementing the original 8 *Keys to Safe Trauma Recovery,* this practical and instructional workbook provides readers an individualized, self-paced 'how to' manual for healing. Empowering the reader's agency, the authors present each idea and intervention with the caveat 'with permission' or 'by invitation only,' which I find very appealing and very Gestalt! The authors' gentle voice and encouraging tone supports the reader in choosing to put the book down quite often in order to do the many powerful experiential exercises offered."

—**Linda A. Curran**, BCPC, LPC, CAACD, CCDPD, and author of
Trauma Competency: A Clinician's Guide and
101 Trauma-Informed Interventions

T0277246

8 KEYS TO SAFE TRAUMA RECOVERY

WORKBOOK

8 Keys to Mental Health Series
Babette Rothschild, Series Editor

The 8 Keys series of books provides consumers with brief, inexpensive, and high-quality self-help books on a variety of topics in mental health. Each volume is written by an expert in the field, someone who is capable of presenting evidence-based information in a concise and clear way. These books stand out by offering consumers cutting-edge, relevant theory in easily digestible portions, written in an accessible style. The tone is respectful of the reader and the messages are immediately applicable. Filled with exercises and practical strategies, these books empower readers to help themselves.

8 KEYS TO SAFE TRAUMA RECOVERY
WORKBOOK

Babette Rothschild

Vanessa Bear

Norton Professional Books

An Imprint of W. W. Norton & Company
Celebrating a Century of Independent Publishing

This book is a general information resource for people who have experienced trauma. It is not a substitute for medical or psychological diagnosis, treatment or therapeutic support for trauma survivors. If you are in danger right now, please seek safety immediately. If you are experiencing a mental health or physical emergency, please go to your nearest emergency room. This book is written to survivors of trauma as defined among these pages. If you suffer from any additional mental health condition concurrent with trauma, such as (but not limited to) suicidality, traumatic brain injury, or psychosis, even though some of the exercises in this book may be helpful to you, advice for managing those conditions are completely beyond the scope of this book. If you have any physical limitations, please consult your healthcare provider before attempting the physical exercises described in this book and follow the instructions given for each exercise carefully, since even simple stretching can cause injuries if it is performed incorrectly or inappropriately.

The patients and their courses of treatment described in this book are composites. Any URLs displayed in this book link or refer to websites that existed as of press time. The publisher is not responsible for, and should not be deemed to endorse or recommend, any website, app, or other content that it did not create. The authors, also, are not responsible for any third-party material.

For information about permission to reproduce selections from this book, write to Permissions, W. W. Norton & Company, Inc., 500 Fifth Avenue, New York, NY 10110

For information about special discounts for bulk purchases, please contact W. W. Norton Special Sales at specialsales@wwnorton.com or 800-233-4830

Manufacturing by Versa Press
Production manager: Gwen Cullen

ISBN: 9781324020127

W. W. Norton & Company, Inc., 500 Fifth Avenue, New York, NY 10110
www.wwnorton.com

W. W. Norton & Company Ltd., 15 Carlisle Street, London W1D 3BS

1 2 3 4 5 6 7 8 9 0

We want to dedicate this book with deep gratitude to the natural world which nourishes us with awe, wonder, and belonging, and to all of the Angels who love and support us: those on the physical plane and those elsewhere.

Contents

Acknowledgments xiii

Introduction xv

KEY 1: **Plotting Your Course With Mindfulness** 1

FIRST, CHECK IN

SOMATIC MARKERS

MINDFUL GAUGE

YOUR MINDFUL GAUGE

PLOT YOUR COURSE

MINDFUL WALKING

BEING HERE, NOW, WITH TASTE

BEING HERE, NOW, WITH SMELL

BEING HERE, NOW, WITH SIGHT

BEING HERE, NOW, WITH SOUND

BEING HERE, NOW, WITH TOUCH

KEY 2: **Begin With Your Epilogue** 32

CURRENT RESOURCES

IDENTIFY YOUR RAINBOWS, AND BRING THEM WITH YOU

TIMELINE

YOUR EPILOGUE

I SURVIVED!

CELEBRATE AND HONOR YOUR SURVIVAL

KEY 3: **Remembering Is Not Required** 54

WHICH PHASE IS MOST USEFUL FOR YOU RIGHT NOW?

TRAUMA TYPES

PROS AND CONS

SAFETY AND STABILITY WISH LIST

ROUTINES AND RITUALS

STABILIZATION BREAKS

SAFE-PLACE MEMORY

WHAT DOES FEELING SAFE AND STABLE MEAN TO YOU?

MAKE A DATE WITH CALM

INCREASING FOCUS AND ATTENTION

CHOOSING THE RIGHT CHAIR

FIND STABILITY THROUGH BALANCE

CREATIVE, CALMING PATTERNS

NOTICING YOUR STABLE BREATH

USING YOUR BREATH TO STABILIZE

KEY 4: **Stop Flashbacks** 104

INTERNAL AND EXTERNAL

SELF-TALK: THAT WAS A MEMORY

MANTRA: THAT WAS A MEMORY

EMPOWER OBJECTS

OTHER ANCHORS TO NOW

PRESENT-DAY FACT SHEET

BEING HERE, NOW KIT

PROTECTIVE BOUNDARIES

DRAW YOUR PROTECTIVE BOUNDARY

FLASHBACK TRIGGERS AND RESOURCES

NOTICING PATTERNS

MAKING A PLAN

TAKING CONTROL OF YOUR FLASHBACK

KEY 5: Reconcile Forgiveness and Shame   136

    Part A: Forgive Your Limitations   136

    AUTONOMIC NERVOUS SYSTEM RESPONSES

    TRAUMA-RESPONSE LIMITATIONS

    ADDITIONAL LIMITATIONS

    SHOULD HAVE, WOULD HAVE, COULD HAVE

    SHALL, WILL, CAN RESOURCES

    FORGIVE-YOUR-LIMITATIONS MANTRA

    FORGIVE-YOUR-LIMITATIONS LETTER

    Part B: Share Your Shame   156

    WHAT IS THE POINT OF SHAME?

    HOW DO YOU KNOW WHEN YOU FEEL SHAME?

    RELIEVE YOUR SHAME

    PUT SHAME BACK WHERE IT BELONGS

    SHARE YOUR SHAME TO CONNECT OR RECONNECT WITH OTHERS

    BE ACCOUNTABLE AND COMPASSIONATE WITH YOURSELF

KEY 6: Take Smaller Steps for Bigger Leaps   184

    REDUCING TO SMALLER STEPS

    RECOVERY GOALS

    SPLITTING ONE GOAL INTO STEPS

    MANAGEABLE STEPS

    GO SLOW

    ALTERNATIVE STEPS

    SUPPORTED STEPS

    ADVOCATING YOUR PACE

KEY 7: Get Moving   210

    FIND YOUR ACTIVITY

    SMALL STEPS AND ALTERNATIVES

    MOVEMENT IN NATURE

    TRY THEM OUT

    FIND AN EXERCISE BUDDY

SET UP RECORD KEEPING

HABIT-MAKING MOVEMENT

TIME-SAVING MOVEMENT HABITS

POSTURE

CONNECTING WITH YOUR STRENGTH

MUSCLE TONING

MOVING WITH BALANCE

KEY 8: **Make Lemonade**   246

WHAT DO I VALUE NOW?

PAY IT FORWARD

HOW TO HELP

KINTSUGI

READY OR NOT?

SMALL STEPS TO LEMONADE

ASSESS YOUR CURRENT COMMITMENT CAPABILITIES

A TRIAL RUN

References   290

Index   293

Acknowledgments

For the most part, we just want to thank each other, Vanessa and Babette, for the wonderful, awesome, easy, warm, good-humored, and on and on experience of writing this book together. We are such a good team, we think we will do another . . . stay tuned!

And we do, also, of course, want to thank our amazing and supportive editor, Deborah Malmud, as well as everyone at W. W. Norton, for seeing (and counseling) us through this project which is also our first experience as coauthors together.

Introduction

Humans have encountered and healed from trauma throughout history and across cultures; from large-scale wars and natural disasters, to devastating traumas in families and neighborhoods. Some of the strategies for healing have evolved via spontaneous instinct and internal wisdom, others have been passed along through generations. Since the last half of the 20th century, interventions have been introduced that are informed by clinical experience, scientific research, and developments in neuroscience. However, one thing is for sure: There is no one-size-fits-all strategy, intervention, or method for healing trauma. Exploring and discovering what is uniquely right for you will be a major factor in your recovery. This workbook will help you identify, assess, and celebrate the resources you already have, and will also offer others that you may find useful to add to your toolbox.

Whether as a direct victim or as a firsthand witness, and regardless of whichever type of trauma is experienced, the reactions of the body and mind are quite similar. The body's nervous system goes into overdrive, and for those who develop posttraumatic stress disorder, those vibrations continue to be felt long after a traumatic event is over. Common reactions include increased vigilance for, and reactiveness to, perceived danger; episodes of anxiety or panic; flashbacks that can fool you into believing you have been transported back to the event; twinges of unease in certain places or situations; and all sorts of disquieting body symptoms that make it difficult to concentrate, disturb sleep and digestion, and on and on. As a result, survivors of trauma might find it difficult to connect with all or part of their body and emotions or to other people. It may feel as though the rug has been pulled from underneath them or that something is just not quite as it should be.

For those whose traumatic experience is in the past, a good starting point is to recognize that you survived. And here is one piece of evidence for that: If you had not survived, you could not be reading this book. Recognizing you survived is also strengthened by learning to notice when your mind and body are *reacting to a memory* of danger, as opposed to *experiencing actual present* danger. This will help you to develop the ability to separate a memory from what is really happening right now. It is our* aim that this book will help you to recognize your survival and gain tools to recover from your trauma, including helping to ease and even heal your ongoing symptoms.

This workbook is a supplement to 8 *Keys to Safe Trauma Recovery*, written by Babette Rothschild in 2010. It is aimed at complementing and enriching that initial volume. The original book offered theory drawn from neuroscience and psychotherapy along with empowering strategies to take charge of healing from trauma. The two books are meant to supplement each other; however, it is not necessary to have read the original to benefit from this workbook. The main difference between this and the original is that here you will find more practical exercises and activities, while the original focuses more on theory. In both books, the eight keys that are integral to safe trauma recovery are explored through various activities aimed at helping you feel safe, stable, and in control of your mind, body, and life, in the aftermath of trauma.

Healing From Trauma Should Not Be Traumatic

This workbook does *not* subscribe to the old motto "No pain, no gain." On the contrary, it is our belief that healing from trauma should not be traumatic. Of course, you may sometimes be rocked by the echoes of what happened in the past; however, the intention of this book is to

---

*Whenever you see "we," "us," or "our," it is referring to the two authors of this book: Babette Rothschild and Vanessa Bear.

decrease the impact of those experiences so that you can enjoy a better quality of life now.

Safety is paramount. During trauma, and in its aftermath, your ability to know what is safe or not can become distorted or difficult to identify. This can happen during recovery too. For example, you may embark on a process of exploring a trauma memory and suddenly become overwhelmed with emotion or lose touch with your surroundings and the present time. For many, it may be detrimental to the healing process to regularly revisit the details of traumatic events. That is the reason that in this workbook we emphasize the importance of building a foundation of stability and resilience, which includes the ability to distinguish the past from the present and to notice what feels safe and what does not. Activities in this book are developed from, and informed by, our clinical experience and are supported by neuroscience, psychology, and somatic psychology. The exercises within each of the eight keys differ in their approach, offering explorations of creativity, movement, mindful awareness, nature connection, visualization, and writing. We hope you find a diverse offering to nourish the diverse parts of you. Please do *not* expect to find every exercise or approach appealing to you. We are endeavoring to provide a broad range of experiences to explore and carefully choose from. By the end of the book, you should have collected a set of tools that are individually tailored to your needs. Do not expect your toolkit to look like anybody else's.

Book Structure

The contents of this workbook follow the same outline as the original *8 Keys to Safe Trauma Recovery* book.

In this book, each "key" chapter contains:

* an explanation of the key's theme, illustrated with one or more examples
* a brief theoretical overview
* discussion of the purpose of that chapter's exercises
* five to 10 exercises linked to that key

- guidelines to evaluate which activities were helpful and to strategize when and where they will be most useful to you
- a plan for how to (or not to) use that key

As this is a workbook, the theory will be brief. If you would like a deeper explanation or understanding of any of the topics, reading the original may offer additional food for thought, but it is not necessary for utilizing this workbook companion. For some of you this will be interesting and help you gain stability through knowledge. However, as with all parts of this book, if the theory does not interest you or provokes you, feel free to skip it. Even though you may find it best to read and apply each key out of order, it may be useful to read Key 1 first. That one lays a foundation for the rest of the book, which may help you decide which key to read next, and so on. Below is an overview of the main points covered in each Key.

KEY 1: PLOTTING YOUR COURSE WITH MINDFULNESS

- Develop awareness and become mindful of body sensations, feelings, and thoughts
- Distinguish pleasant sensations, feelings, and thoughts from those that are unpleasant
- Learn to hold your attention on what is happening right now
- Use mindfulness to discover your personal Mindful Gauge

KEY 2: BEGIN WITH YOUR EPILOGUE

- Acknowledge that the traumatic event is over and that time has passed since (if indeed it is and it has)
- Confirm you survived

KEY 3: REMEMBERING IS NOT REQUIRED

- Identify your current level of stability and quality of life
- Evaluate whether reviewing traumatic memories is useful for you or not
- Gain alternatives to reviewing memories and tools to feel more stable

KEY 4: STOP FLASHBACKS

- Differentiate triggers from events
- Separate memory of the past from the present
- Use your senses to identify safety and danger

KEY 5A: FORGIVE YOUR LIMITATIONS

- Understand and accept that during trauma, control is taken away from you
- Explore the importance of contact and support

KEY 5B: SHARE YOUR SHAME

- Assign an honest balance of responsibility
- Understand, accept, and resolve shame resulting from trauma

KEY 6: TAKE SMALLER STEPS FOR BIGGER LEAPS

- Learn how "slow and steady" often makes for a quicker road to recovery from trauma
- Gain permission to reach goals at a pace that ensures success
- Embrace and redefine "avoidance"

KEY 7: GET MOVING

- Be able to antidote the freeze response
- Increase containment, self and body control, and muscle tone
- Dissipate and regulate stress

KEY 8: MAKE LEMONADE

- Find meaning in your experiences
- Turn adversity into advantage
- Identify activities and projects that will broaden your attention to the world
- Counter the effects of trauma by being active and useful

You Are in the Driver's Seat

The exercises in this book have been chosen based on those that have been useful for us, our clients, and clients of those we teach and supervise. However, no exercise will suit everyone, so do not expect every exercise to appeal to or work for you. In addition, in no way are you obliged or expected to do them all. When you read through one, notice how it lands. If it sounds and feels good, try it. Make sure to continue to notice how you feel in your body, emotions, and thoughts as you do an exercise. Then evaluate, and keep only the ones that feel right and toss out the ones that do not. You can use a few, many, or all of the tools, and you can use them alongside other self-help activities that you have found or will find to be beneficial.

We encourage you, actually implore you, to be picky. Channel your inner Goldilocks and identify what feels "just right" to help you to recover from trauma. The Mindful Gauge and activities in Key 1 may help you with this; that is the reason we placed that key first.

You may find that different exercises are useful or not, at different times. What feels right today might not be right tomorrow, and vice versa. Therefore, regular check-ins are recommended. When something does not feel right, consider whether it might be something to keep in your back pocket, to try again at another time. By experimenting with different exercises in various combinations and time frames, you will find the ones that work best for you, and the situations they are most suited to.

All activities have been carefully chosen and described with an eye to avoiding trigger responses. However, if you do feel more triggered, rather than more stable, it may be a sign that an activity is not a good fit for you, at least at that moment.

Will It Work?

Hopefully this workbook will assist in your recovery. However, it is not meant to be a treatment program in itself. A question we are often asked is whether it is possible to heal from trauma. The experience of one of the authors, Vanessa, may help answer this question. Her healing had come to an impasse until she met someone who, like herself, had experienced flashbacks, panic, and difficulties self-regulating for many years. This person had overcome these symptoms to the point of hardly experiencing them at all anymore. Simply finding out that someone else had been able to change meant that the possibility suddenly became real for Vanessa. That lit a light at the end of her long recovery tunnel. It took many resources and some effort to find her way through, but knowing it was possible gave her a light to follow.

So, yes, it is absolutely possible to recover from trauma, and to have a better quality of life. But recovery looks different for each individual. You may or may not continue to feel the vibrations or shadows of what happened to you. Either way, you can definitely become equipped to cope, to focus on the present, to take control, and to recognize any remaining vibrations as memories, rather than feeling as though you are experiencing the trauma again. History cannot be changed and the experiences you have had will not be erased, but the good news is that you have already survived them. In recognizing your survival and engaging in your healing, you will be different in some ways; in particular, you will be more robust and better resourced.

Sometimes trauma survivors experience a feeling like regressing. It can happen if you become triggered unexpectedly or an event in daily life gets in the way. However, the more you visit that feeling with increased tools to cope, the easier it will be to get back. Eventually you will create a superhighway that enables you to get yourself back quickly and confidently to a feeling of stability. You will also begin to notice that the time lag between getting triggered and getting back to calm and the present moment gradually gets shorter. That will be a sure sign that you are in the process of healing.

Disclaimer

What we share in this book is based on experience, theory, and informed speculation. There is nothing in the field of psychology or trauma treatment that is hard fact, and very little in science or medicine. Knowledge and understanding of trauma, the brain, the body, and the universe changes and evolves all the time. Additionally, one approach or exercise will not have the same effect for every person. What helps one person may not another, and vice versa. That said, the exercises shared here are founded on well-researched practices and theories that we have found to be effective for many. Some are likely to be useful to you, but do not expect them all to be.

You may feel some disappointment that there is not one fix-all approach to your recovery from trauma. The good news, however, is that you are the expert on you. We feel that one of the greatest tools you have, and can develop using some tools in this book, is to recognize what feels right for and helps *you*. With this awareness you can decide on, and tailor, the tools of your recovery to best suit your individual needs.

8 KEYS TO SAFE TRAUMA RECOVERY

WORKBOOK

KEY 1 PLOTTING YOUR COURSE WITH MINDFULNESS

Decision-making touches just about every aspect of daily life. You choose the time you get up, what you wear, what you eat; you choose your friends, partner, work, home, and so on. Of course, some decisions are straightforward, and others involve varying degrees of complexity. You may have already discovered, along with many others who have suffered trauma, that it is difficult to make certain decisions, sometimes even ones that appear to be simple. Being better equipped for decision-making will increase your feeling of self-control in many aspects of your life. The mindful approach in this chapter will help you to, among other things, choose which healing tools belong in your unique toolbox, as well as give you more confidence for choosing your helpers and healing path.

Simple mindfulness can (among other things) provide a solid foundation for decision-making. It can help you make informed decisions about your healing, such as which therapist is the right one for you, or which technique is most likely to be beneficial. It can also help you determine when you need to adapt a situation to avoid becoming overwhelmed. Mindful awareness has the potential to put you back in the driver's seat of your life.

The concept and practice of mindfulness stems back through Hindu and Buddhist traditions for thousands of years. It is also thought to have roots in Judaism, Christianity, and Islam (Trousselard et al., 2014). Of course, mindfulness has not existed solely within religious activities. In fact, for many decades, mindfulness has been increasingly popular as a secular practice throughout the world. This book will stick to the benefits of the functional (nonreligious) aspects of mindfulness as related

1

to increasing self-awareness and focusing on what is happening in the present, from moment to moment.

Though it is often used in meditation, mindfulness itself is not meditation. You do not need training to be able to be mindful, nor do you need to subscribe to a religion or philosophy. Mindfulness is, simply, the practice of observing what is happening at any given moment without judging what you observe. That includes awareness of your body sensations, your surroundings, your emotional state, the thoughts and images in your mind, and so on.

Are you wondering what mindfulness is not? The opposite of being mindful is like being on autopilot. For example, you may have had the experience of driving somewhere without actually remembering how you got there. Or maybe you have eaten a meal while watching a TV show and been surprised to suddenly find that your plate is empty but you do not remember how the food tasted. Being on autopilot can also prevent you from noticing body sensations that tell you when you are hungry or when you have eaten enough. Moreover, it can decrease your skills for evaluating others by recognizing facial expressions and other cues that would help you identify safety (such as a genuine smile) or danger (such as a menacing grimace).

Unlike being on autopilot, when you are mindfully aware in varying combinations of your body sensations, your surroundings, and the thoughts and images in your mind, you become equipped to take stock of your current situation and make decisions on your own behalf.

The exercises in this key will progressively build your capacity to be mindful. They will increase your ability to notice what does and what does not work for you. You will gain skill in identifying foods and activities that help you feel safer and calmer, and lay a foundation for your ability to make decisions of all sorts. There are also exercises to help you use mindfulness to simply feel more grounded in the present moment, which is a good tool to have for anyone who may feel at the mercy of memories from the past. In addition, the skills learned in this Key will help you to determine which exercises this, and all the other, Keys are useful to keep in your tool kit, and which you want to leave out altogether or set aside for now.

FIRST, CHECK IN

In this key you will learn how to utilize a Mindful Gauge to assess your reactions to different choices. This can help you to make effective decisions and weigh your options. For you to be able to assess a reaction, you must first be mindfully aware of where you are starting from.

METHOD

1. Without moving or changing the way you are sitting, lying, or standing, take a moment to notice how you are right now. You may notice your mood, the thoughts or images in your mind, or perhaps something happening in your body.

2. Look through the suggestions in the following table and consider which apply to what is going on for you in this moment. If you experience something else that is not listed here, add it to the "Any Other Noticeable Reactions" section.

> **EXTRA GUIDANCE:** For some people, noticing body sensations is unpleasant or triggering. This exercise, like all in this book, is not meant to overwhelm you or make you feel more uncomfortable. If you feel an unpleasant reaction or feel worse when you notice any of these sensations, stop.

Right now, I notice:

Body sensations	Tight chest	Soft belly	Lengthened spine	Faster heartbeat	Fidgetiness
	Stiffness	Numbness	Soft eyes	Sighing	Holding my breath
	Soft muscles	Cold feet	Steady heartbeat	Pain/aching	Sweatiness
Thoughts, poems, sayings, analogies, songs	I cannot . . .	I love the . . .	I hate . . .	This reminds me of . . .	I wish it were . . .
	I do not like . . .	I am glad it is . . .	I prefer . . .	I do not under-stand . . .	I need to . . .
	Later I will . . .				
Emotions	Angry	Cheerful	Cranky	Frustrated	Excited
	Energized	Peaceful	Uncomfort-able	Sleepy	Sad
	Disgusted	Withdrawn	Revolted	Anxious	Nervous
	Afraid	Cozy	Confused	Satisfied	
Mind's images— memories of smells, tastes, sounds, sights, inner impulses	*Draw or describe any image(s) in your mind right now.*				
Any other noticeable reactions					

SOMATIC MARKERS

Antonio Damasio's somatic marker theory (Damasio, 1994) suggests that our life experiences leave reactions or markers in our body. For example, if Vanessa smells hot doughnuts, she feels how her facial expression changes, her lips turn up, she notices a warm sensation in her belly, and her mood shifts to feeling happy. The smell of hot doughnuts reminds Vanessa of long summer days as a young child exploring the sandy cove she went to during the holidays. The delicious smell of fried doughnuts from the beachside café wafted down the beach. Those memories have embedded a reaction to the experiences in her body and emotions.

Awareness of these emotional and body reactions is a built-in mechanism for decision-making. We all create somatic markers, usually unconsciously, all the time. They are the basis for all our decisions whether we know it or not. That is why sometimes you will have an attraction or aversion to something without necessarily understanding (or maybe even thinking about) why. Below are some ways to make your somatic markers conscious so that you will be able to use them at will to your advantage.

METHOD
Practice 1

1. Choose a favorite food.
2. Remember eating that food at some time in the past.
3. See if you can recall the smell, texture, taste of that food.
4. Compare your memory of how that food felt while you were eating it to what you feel *now* as you remember it. What is the sensation in your stomach? Do you feel an emotion? Is your mouth watering or changing expression? Those reactions you have now while you are remembering are the somatic markers connected to that food for you.
5. Jot down any body or emotional responses to this pleasant memory.

Practice 2

1. Recall a favorite place, person, or animal. For this practice, make sure you choose a *pleasant* memory that is not connected to grief or trauma.

2. Develop that "image" of the place, person, or animal in your mind to remember the details.

    If it is a favorite place, what do you remember hearing when you were there? What do you remember seeing? Smelling? Doing?

    If you chose a favorite person, what do you remember about how they looked? What was their typical facial expression and body language? Is there an activity you remember them doing?

    If you chose an animal, what do you remember about how they moved? What do you remember about how they looked? If you remember touching them, how did that feel?

3. As you recall this memory, notice whether you have any response *right now, in the present*. Do you notice any change in temperature in your face or any other parts of your body? Does your muscle tone change? Are there sensations in your stomach or changes in your heartbeat or breathing? Are you aware of a change in emotion or mood? Those reactions you have while you are remembering are the somatic markers connected to that person, place, or animal for you.

4. Jot down in the chart any body or emotional responses to this pleasant memory.

> **EXTRA GUIDANCE:** Not everyone will have an image of the food or person/place/animal in their mind. Everyone experiences memories in a different way. If you are struggling, it might help to look at a photograph if you have one.

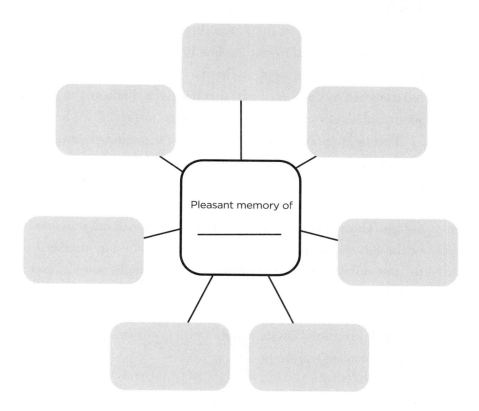

Pleasant memory of

_____

MINDFUL GAUGE

GOLDILOCKS, OUR GAUGE ROLE MODEL

You likely know the story of Goldilocks and the Three Bears, but here is a quick summary: Goldilocks was on a walk in a forest when she found a house with its door open. When she went inside, she found three bowls of porridge on the table. She tasted the first and found it was too hot, the second was too cold, the third was just right. She ate all of the third bowlful. Then, she went to sit down. The first chair she tried was too big, the second too small, the third was just right. Then, she went upstairs to find a bed to rest in. The first bed was too hard, the second too soft, the third just right. In the story, Goldilocks is found sleeping in the third bed by the three bears that live there. For you, the point is how adept Goldilocks was at noticing what was "just right" for her.

Paying attention to your response to something (somatic markers along with other types of reactions) will help you to identify whether it has a positive or a negative effect on you. With practice, your mindful awareness can be shaped into your own personal tool, a *Mindful Gauge*. Those reactions you are most aware of will fall into one or more of the following categories: body sensations (somatic markers), images in your mind (memories in pictures, or of smells, sounds, and so on), mood (emotions), and thoughts (including anything with words: a song, a poem, an analogy, a statement, and such). To make best use of your personal Mindful Gauge, simply notice your reactions; do not try to change or adapt your response.

Nadifa practiced developing her own Mindful Gauge. She began with benign choices, such as in the exercise below. She identified her most reliable Mindful Gauges as physical sensations in her chest and neck. When something was unpleasant, she noticed her neck would feel hot and her chest tight. When something was pleasant, she noticed her chest and neck were relaxed and at normal temperature.

When her friend invited her on a shopping trip, Nadifa was nervous about getting overwhelmed as she often did in those types of situations, but she very much wanted to shop with her friend. So, before the trip she prepared herself by finding images online of the different stores they might visit. When looking at the online pictures of the mall, she felt hot and tight in the chest, suggesting to her that the mall might not be the best place to visit right now. However, when she looked at the photos of the boutique her friend most wanted to visit, Nadifa felt soft in her chest and no heat in her neck. In the end, she and her friend successfully went to the boutique and not the mall. By using her mindful gauge before the trip Nadifa was able to assess her options and make an informed decision about the best place for the shopping trip with her friend.

Jeffrey drove his wife crazy at restaurants because he could never decide what to order. He would choose one thing and then call the waiter back to choose something different. He often broke out in a cold sweat. Both he and his wife dreaded eating out together. Eventually, however, Jeffrey was able to change his restaurant indecision. At home he would practice mindfully choosing different food items throughout his day: orange versus apple, cereal versus eggs, coffee versus tea, and so on. It took him some days, but eventually he realized he could rely on three gauges: (1) whether his breathing quickened or slowed; (2) whether he noticed a subtle change in his mood (toward happy or sad); and (3) when he listened, he often heard a clear "no" or "yes" in his head. He future-tested his gauges with visits on his own to a coffee bar and sometimes to a fast-food joint for lunch. When he felt ready, he invited his wife out to a restaurant for dinner. His wife knew what he had been practicing, so kept quiet while he perused the menu. He drew on his Mindful Gauges and was able to decide on the meal he wanted the first time, with no regret. It worked for dessert too.

Nadifa's and Jeffrey's experiences are just two examples of successful uses of the Mindful Gauge. Take note that both of them practiced and prepared their gauges before attempting to rely on them. So, make sure to give yourself time to identify and develop your own Mindful Gauge or gauges. As they did, try using different gauges for benign choices, that is, choices that have little or no stress attached, to help you identify which gauges give you the most consistent and reliable information.

Honing your awareness with less significant choices will help you tackle more difficult decisions later with confidence. Choose one of the categories below, or something else benign, to make a choice between, and channel your inner Goldilocks.

METHOD

1. Find two options to choose from. For example, an apple and a banana, or a striped and a plain sock, or one TV show and another.

> Which socks to wear

or

> Which fruit to eat

or

> Which TV show to watch

2. Using the following table, choose one of the gauges (at a time) to practice with. You could use the same options for each gauge, but be sure to practice different gauges at separate times. You might experience something not suggested in the table at all; it is impossible to list here all of the likely responses you may notice. These are solely suggestions rather than what should happen.

3. Focus on one of the options above (e.g., striped sock), and write down your responses.

   There are some examples within each category, and spaces for you to write your own.

   Then, focus on the other option (e.g., plain sock), and note down your responses to that.

   If it is an object or food, rather than an activity, you might want to use your senses to help: smell it, touch it.

4. Notice which of the two options gave the most pleasant and least pleasant reactions.

5. Then make your choice based on the most pleasant reaction and see if it elicits the response you expected. For example, if you chose an apple, take a bite and see if it tasted as good as your gauge suggested. If you want, you can also taste the banana to see whether that really would have been the wrong choice.

6. When you have completed this for several trials, reflect on which gauge or gauges gave you the most reliable information. Those will be your Mindful Gauges that you can use in the future.

7. You can return to this exercise one or more times in the future to check whether your Mindful Gauge or gauges are the same or whether they have changed. Or you may discover that specific gauges work for particular types of choices so that you shift between different ones depending on the task.

	OPTION 1			OPTION 2	
Body sensations	Tight chest	Soft belly	Lengthened spine	Faster heartbeat	Fidgetiness
	Stiffness	Numbness	Soft eyes	Sighing	Holding my breath
	Soft muscles	Cold feet	Steady heartbeat	Pain/aching	Sweatiness
Thoughts, poems, sayings, analogies, songs	I cannot do it	I love the . . .	I hate it	This reminds me of . . .	I wish it were . . .
	I do not like . . .	I am glad it is . . .	I prefer . . .	I do not under-stand . . .	I need to . . .
	Later I will . . .				
Emotions	Angry	Cheerful	Cranky	Frustrated	Excited
	Energized	Peaceful	Uncomfort-able	Sleepy	Sad
	Disgusted	Withdrawn	Revolted	Anxious	Nervous
	Afraid	Cozy	Confused	Satisfied	

Mind's images—memories of smells, tastes, sounds, sights, inner impulses	OPTION 1 *Draw or describe **any** image(s) that come to mind when you focus your attention on this option.*	OPTION 2 *Draw or describe **any** image(s) that come to mind when you focus your attention on this option.*
Any other noticeable reactions		

YOUR MINDFUL GAUGE

The more you practice using and noticing your Mindful Gauge, the more of an expert you will become.

METHOD

1. Looking back over the previous two exercises, pick out the response or responses that gave you the most reliable information.
2. For the next week, use those gauges to notice your responses to inconsequential decisions you make, such as which shirt to wear or what to eat for your evening meal.
3. Record the decisions you made using the Mindful Gauge and also whether it gave a reliable indication for you. Different Mindful Gauges may work better with different types of decisions. For example, you might find that a body sensation is most reliable with food choices, or a change in mood is a more reliable gauge with choices relating to people.
4. Record how reliable each gauge is. You may notice that one is more reliable than another, or you may notice a response you have not listed.

> **EXTRA GUIDANCE:** Use the "First, Check In" exercise at the start of this Key before you make the decision, so that you can more easily notice the actual response to the decision itself. For example, if Nadifa's neck had already felt hot before she made her choice, it would have been difficult to assess the effectiveness of her Mindful Gauge. Noticing the sensation in her neck beforehand enabled her to determine whether looking at the image of the shop had caused a change.

Mindful gauge: _____

MINDFUL GAUGE RESPONSE	The decision I was making	Record how effective it was in helping you make the "just right" decision (1 = not effective at all, 5 = very effective)				
		1	2	3	4	5
		1	2	3	4	5
		1	2	3	4	5
		1	2	3	4	5

Mindful gauge: _____

MINDFUL GAUGE RESPONSE	The decision I was making	Record how effective it was in helping you make the "just right" decision (1 = not effective at all, 5 = very effective)				
		1	2	3	4	5
		1	2	3	4	5
		1	2	3	4	5
		1	2	3	4	5

Mindful gauge: _____

MINDFUL GAUGE RESPONSE	The decision I was making	Record how effective it was in helping you make the "just right" decision (1 = not effective at all, 5 = very effective)				
		1	2	3	4	5
		1	2	3	4	5
		1	2	3	4	5
		1	2	3	4	5

PLOT YOUR COURSE

Using your Mindful Gauge to plot your course through this book might be a way to start feeling in control. When embarking on a healing and therapy journey you may find yourself faced with a myriad of therapeutic approaches and techniques to choose from. This can feel daunting. Using your Mindful Gauge, you can get into the driver's seat of your recovery and follow the course that feels right for you.

METHOD

1. From the previous exercise, choose one or two of the most prominent or most reliable gauges.
2. Read through the chapter headings and descriptions listed in the table one at a time.
3. Notice whether there are any responses from your Mindful Gauge to what you have read, and write them down. You may wish to mark the level of reaction on the scale so that you can compare each chapter. There may be some you feel drawn toward and some that you feel an adverse reaction to.
4. Look through the list and your responses. Number the order that you will take through the book. Choose the ones that had the most pleasant reaction to read first. If you had an adverse reaction to any it may be a sign not to read that one yet, or to read it but not to feel you need to do any of those exercises at the moment. Remember, you can always reject an exercise now and return to it later or not at all.
5. You might like to add the numbers of the keys to this roadmap as a reminder of what order you are going to read them in. Leave out the ones you do not want to read at the moment. When you have finished, notice how it feels to look at it. Which aspects of your Mindful Gauge are activated? Notice whether there is anything about the order you would like to change, and feel free to change it at any time.

> **EXTRA GUIDANCE:** Keep returning to your Mindful Gauge to evaluate each plan, exercise, tool, and Key. Use the gauge to assess whether any therapeutic approach and technique, or therapist, is right for you.

KEYS	Mindful Gauge reaction	Order in which to read this book
KEY 1: Plotting Your Course With Mindfulness • Develop awareness and become mindful of body sensations, feelings, and thoughts • Distinguish pleasant from unpleasant • Be able to focus on what is happening right now • Use mindfulness to discover your individual Mindful Gauge		
KEY 2: Begin With Your Epilogue • Acknowledge it is over (if it is) and time has passed since • You survived		
KEY 3: Remembering Is Not Required • Evaluate current stability/quality of life • Evaluate whether going over traumatic memories is useful or not • Feel more stable		
KEY 4: Stop Flashbacks • Differentiate triggers from events • Distinguish memory from present • Use your senses to gain external information about the present and separate that information from the reactions and sensations of your body		
KEY 5: Reconcile Forgiveness and Shame • Find an honest balance of responsibility • Understand and accept that during trauma, control is taken away from you; that you were unable to stop what happened (or, if it was you that caused/perpetrated it, face up to regret, and decide if reparation may first be necessary) • Explore the importance of getting contact instead of isolating or withdrawing • Understand, accept, and resolve shame resulting from trauma		

KEYS	Mindful Gauge reaction	Order in which to read this book
KEY 6: Take Smaller Steps for Bigger Leaps • "Slow and steady" often makes for a much quicker road to recovery from trauma • Reach goals, and have permission to do so slowly • Notice avoidance and develop "permission" to use the gauge to try something more appropriate for you		
KEY 7: Get Moving • Antidote to freeze response • Increase containment, self-control, and muscle tone • Dissipate and regulate stress		
KEY 8: Make Lemonade • Find meaning in your experience • Turn adversity into advantage, helping or advocating for others (if it DECREASES your symptoms) • Begin activities and projects that will give you something else to think about other than your trauma • Be inspired and energized and counter the effects of trauma by being active and useful		

MINDFUL WALKING

Recovering from trauma can be tiring. You have the added challenge of having to manage all the general tasks of everyday life alongside managing your symptoms and finding ways to heal. The discipline of mindfulness can offer varying degrees of respite from many symptoms, including intrusive thoughts, flashbacks, worries, and so on. Some people find taking extra naps, self-massage, or meditation restful. Others, however, find typical relaxation practices difficult (which will be discussed at greater length in Key 7), with jitters coming to the surface and their mind racing even more. For these and other reasons, mindful walking could be a useful practice. Of course, use your Mindful Gauge to decide whether you want to try this now, later, or not at all, and if you do try it, to evaluate its usefulness for you. Use your five senses to hold your awareness in the present and to be aware of your current surroundings as you walk.

METHOD

Choose a pleasant place to do your mindful walking. This could be in a park, beach, or woodland, or in your own home. Ideally, select a place that your Mindful Gauge tells you already brings you a feeling of calm or, at the least, does not produce an unpleasant reaction. Mindful walking does not need to be for the purpose of fitness. Use your Mindful Gauge to decide what speed and length of walk brings most calmness, and keep checking in as you walk.

> **EXTRA GUIDANCE:** Choose one of the options below to use at a time. Maybe use an option for a set number of minutes, or steps, or for your whole walk. Are there any other ways you could find focus?
>
> You can apply these mindful walking exercises to any type of movement. If you find movement a good resource, Key 7 includes more options.

OPTION 1

Notice the surface under your feet and how it changes as you walk. Feel the texture under the soles of your shoes. What textures do you notice? How does stony or hard or soft ground feel underfoot?

OPTION 2

As you walk, notice your body. What is the shape of your spine as you walk? Straight, bent, curved? How does your balance shift as you lift one foot and lower it to the ground?

OPTION 3

Count your steps to three: "1. 2. 3, 1. 2. 3," and so on. Whenever your mind wanders to something else and you lose track of counting, congratulate yourself for noticing you lost track, and start again!

OPTION 4

In your mind or aloud recite one or more words that have meaning for you. Babette sometimes chants "Healthier, stronger, calmer, fitter" as she mindfully walks. What would be your words, if any?

OPTION 5

1. Go for a walk outside for 5–20 minutes several days this week. Use your Mindful Gauge to decide frequency and duration.

2. Before setting off, consider a route you could take that you expect to be pleasant. Use your Mindful Gauge to decide which route to take.

3. You might also want to use the "First, Check In" exercise so that you are aware of how you are feeling before your walk.

4. During the walk, as much as possible, be mindfully aware of your experiences. You might want to choose a sensory theme for the walk, such as to be mostly aware of what you hear or what you see.

5. After the walk, write or draw about your experience. Include what you saw or heard or felt. You might want to use the space below, or use a journal.

6. At the end of the week, read back through your journal, noticing how you feel as you read. Did your writing reflect awareness from a particular sense? Did your mood on that day affect what you noticed and wrote about on your walk? Did you notice similar or different things? Did you feel better or worse after your walk? Is this something that would be beneficial to add to your daily routine?

WALKING JOURNAL

Monday

Tuesday

Wednesday

Thursday

Friday

Saturday

Sunday

Training Your Mind to Keep Your Attention in the Present Time

The following set of exercises uses your five senses to help you cultivate a grounded connection to the here and now. Often, survivors of trauma experience flashbacks or intrusive memories that can cause them to lose connection with the present moment. Training that connection to the present when you are not overwhelmed can help you access it more easily when you really need it.

BEING HERE, NOW, WITH TASTE

Though this exercise is focused on taste, it actually engages most of the senses: looking at the piece of food, smelling it, feeling the texture against your fingers and the insides of your mouth, and, of course, tasting it.*

METHOD

Experiment with different foods; maybe something sour brings you more awareness, or maybe choose a food that you associate with a comforting memory.

1. First, use your Mindful Gauge (body, mind, emotion) to check in with how you are feeling right now.
2. Take a piece of chocolate, or, if you are allergic to or do not like chocolate, take a small piece of something else that melts, that you would find pleasant to eat.
3. Hold it in the palm of your hand, notice its shape and texture.
4. Notice any sensations in your body, such as your mouth starting to water.
5. Hold it to your nose and smell it, noticing any response from your Mindful Gauge as you do.
6. Place it in your mouth, without chewing. Notice the texture and taste.
7. Move it around the mouth and notice how it feels and tastes as you move it.
8. If it's chocolate, let it melt in your mouth, continuing to notice the changing texture and taste. With a raisin, allow it to soften and then start to gently chew it, noticing the taste and texture as you do.
9. Notice how it feels as you swallow, and the taste left in your mouth.
10. How long does the taste of it stay in your mouth?

* As inspired by John Kabat-Zinn (2013) in his book, *Full Catastrophe Living*.

BEING HERE, NOW, WITH SMELL

Scientists have discovered that information from the sense of smell travels faster to your brain than the other senses. This means that smells can be very potent. Do you recall a time when a particular smell evoked a strong emotion connected to something that happened in the past?

The smell of cookies baking makes Vanessa feel calmer. She notices a feeling of warmth in her belly and an image in her mind of her dear friend Alice welcoming her into her warm home for tea. Also, the smell of mint helps her to focus, feel alert, and connect to the here and now very quickly. Those are key smells for Vanessa. Yours may be quite different.

Notice which scents bring you to the present and which invoke pleasant memories or a feeling of calm. Keep track of those kinds of effects, as each signals a resource that might be useful in different situations.

METHOD

1. Choose one or more scents from around your home. Perfumes, flowers, spices, herbs, and so on are possible choices. You might also consider a favorite soft toy or blanket, the soap or shampoo you use, a food item in your cupboard or refrigerator. Take some time to sniff each scent one at a time. For the purpose of this exercise, stick to those that evoke pleasant feelings and memories. If there are one or more odors you are averse to, or already know it evokes bad memories for you, set it aside for now.

2. Use your Mindful Gauge to notice how you feel before smelling each scent. Then use it again to notice how you feel afterward.

A scent that invokes a pleasant memory	A scent that connects you to the here and now
_____	_____

3. Notice the response from your Mindful Gauge when you smell the pleasant memory scent.

4. Notice the response from your Mindful Gauge when you smell the scent that makes you feel pleasantly alert.

5. If you identify one or more scents that help you feel calm, as that of fresh-baked cookies does for Vanessa, you might keep something with that scent with you. Maybe a cinnamon stick, a small vial of your perfume or shampoo, a lemon candy, and so on. If it is something that can spoil, make sure to replace it regularly. That way you will have a tool available to you at any time to call your attention into the present and help you feel calmer.

BEING HERE, NOW, WITH SIGHT

Often, when people feel triggered, their body moves into a startle response where they become frozen and stiff, afraid to move or look around. By moving your head and your eyes to look around and check for danger and safety, you can break out of that pattern.

METHOD

1. Standing or sitting, move your head slowly in different directions, as feels comfortable for you. Remember to move your eyes too.
2. Look above you, below you, and all around you, noticing and naming what you *actually* see (as opposed to what you expect to see).

Choose simple things to notice and name:

- Identify various colors you see, *or*
- Pick a single color you find soothing and notice the places where you find it in your surroundings, *or*
- Pay attention to the shapes of the objects you see, *or*
- Notice the shadows and where you can see streams of light, *or*
- Count how many light sources you see, *or*
- Find and trace with your eyes the corners and edges of different things you see, *or*
- Attend to the facial expressions of the people around you.
- Choose just one of these options at a time; do not try to do them all at once.

> **EXTRA GUIDANCE:** Notice whether there is one type of thing that feels easier to hold your focus, as well as noticing whether there is a category that you find distressing or unnerving. For example, if a particular color triggers an unpleasant reaction for you, choose to look for something other than that color.

BEING HERE, NOW, WITH SOUND

This exercise can be done in just a minute or so to quickly reorient and ground yourself. You can sit down or stand up for this exercise.

METHOD

1. Notice the farthest-away sound you can hear—traffic, a barking dog, the hum of the refrigerator, and so on.
2. Notice the pitch of that sound and whether it is continuous or broken.
3. Identify what direction it is coming from.
4. Then turn your attention to the closest sound you are aware of.
5. Identify and name what is making that sound.
6. Alternate your awareness between the farthest and nearest sounds. Then see if it is possible to hear both at the same time.

OTHER SOUND RESOURCES (add your own to the list):

- Carry headphones to listen to music that you find calming or uplifting. Maybe make a playlist to listen to when you need it. Dancing or singing along can be great too.
- For some people, listening to their own breath is calming.
- Clap your hands or stamp your feet.
- Listen to the sound of your own voice.
- Record a loved one, or yourself, saying reassuring and encouraging things about you.

- _____
- _____

BEING HERE, NOW, WITH TOUCH

Feeling the texture of an object can help focus your attention in the present moment.

METHOD

1. Choose an object that looks appealing. Maybe a leaf, an item of clothing, a rock, an ornament, or such.
2. Move your hands lightly over the surface of the object, noticing the sensations at your fingertips.
3. Trace the edges of the object, noticing whether the sensation is different or the same.
4. Rub parts of the object between your fingers and thumb and notice whether it feels the same on your fingers as it does on your thumb. Observe how it feels to hold it with both hands and whether the sensation is the same.
5. Identify whether the object and different parts of the object feel soft, warm, firm, cold, smooth, textured, or spiky.
6. Notice whether there is a touch sensation you would like to feel that is not present with this object. Look around to see if there is another object nearby that could create that sensation.
7. If there is an object that feels particularly potent at bringing you into the present moment, make a note of it in your resources list to remind you, or carry it with you.

Key Review

Did you remember to use your Mindful Gauge to evaluate the exercises in this chapter? If not, was that by choice or because you forgot?

	Did this exercise help, or make you feel worse?	If it helped, what reaction did you have that told you it helped? (For example, felt calmer or stronger or more present.)
First, Check In		
Somatic Markers		
Mindful Gauge		
Your Mindful Gauge		
Plot Your Course		
Mindful Walking		

If you forgot, consider whether you want to go back and do that.

Once you have completed an exercise you may wish to jot down your response and its effectiveness for you in the table.

If it helped, could it be adapted to help more? How?	If it helped, when do you plan to use it?	If it did not help, could you change or adapt it to better suit you? How?

	Did this exercise help, or make you feel worse?	If it helped, what reaction did you have that told you it helped? (For example, felt calmer or stronger or more present.)
Being Here, Now, With Taste		
Being Here, Now, With Smell		
Being Here, Now, With Sight		
Being Here, Now, With Sound		
Being Here, Now, With Touch		

If it helped, could it be adapted to help more? How?	If it helped, when do you plan to use it?	If it did not help, could you change or adapt it to better suit you? How?

KEY 2 BEGIN WITH YOUR EPILOGUE

In storytelling, whether a book, play, or movie, an *epilogue* is a concluding chapter that summarizes events that follow the ending of the story. Usually, the epilogue briefly describes how life went on after the drama ended. For example, at the end of the seventh and last book in the Harry Potter series, the concluding chapter details the final battle to save Hogwarts School. That chapter is then followed by an epilogue that jumps 19 years into the future when Harry is an adult, married, and, among other things, is sending his own children off to their first year at Hogwarts.

Depending on what happened with your trauma, and what is happening in your life now, you may or may not *yet* have an epilogue to your story.

Therefore, please take note: This chapter is *not* for those whose trauma is ongoing. If you are still living daily in a situation of trauma, then you do not, as yet, have an epilogue. In that case, please skip this chapter *for now* and return to it when whatever-it-is has actually ended. That means, for example, a war is over, abuse has stopped (permanently), a natural disaster has abated, and so on, and life has returned to some semblance of "normal." For those of you whose trauma has not ended, please skip to Key 3. For those of you whose trauma has indeed ended, read on.

You may have been told by therapists, self-help books, or friends that recounting or repeatedly reviewing your trauma story will be therapeutic and cathartic. However, as we discuss in detail in the next chapter, for many people telling or ruminating on their story is not a stabilizing process. In fact, too often people end up feeling more overwhelmed by that process. For now, it is worth mentioning that the most important and empowering part of any trauma story is the ending: *the fact that you survived.*

For those who continue to suffer from the effects of trauma, even when many years have passed, it often feels as if their traumatic incident never ended. This is largely due to the way the brain functions during and following trauma, which will be discussed later in this chapter. But first an example:

When Maya was 10, she got separated from her family in a forest while admiring a bird's nest in a tree. As a result, she endured what felt like hours wandering around, desperately trying to find them. She felt abandoned, endangered, and terrified. Now Maya is an adult, but she freaked out when her children came home with a letter from school inviting families on a camping trip in a nearby woodland. Her wife, Sophie, realized how scared Maya still felt when she was in a forest, and offered to take the children on her own. However, Maya really wanted to join her family for that trip.

As part of Maya's recovery process, she and her therapist, Vanessa, decided to use a method from cognitive–behavioral therapy called "in vivo exposure." They walked to a local woodland to explore Maya's feelings and identify ways to help her cope during the upcoming trip. That meant that they actually went to the woodland where she had become upset. They took it very slowly.

In very small steps (Key 6), they exposed Maya to the situation (being in the woods) that she was so frightened of. The first step was just going to, and not in, the woods. As soon as they neared the first path, Maya became panicky. She told Vanessa that she could feel her heart racing and that she felt disoriented. As is typical, her nervous system was remembering how she felt when she was lost as a child. Over the next several sessions they gradually stepped closer to the entrance to the woodland, and then, a bit at a time, took a few steps into the woods. Each step was decided by Maya so that she would feel in control. The one exception was that sometimes Vanessa advised her to take an even smaller step, not to rush it.

In addition to taking smaller steps, as advised in Key 6, they applied some of the exercises from this Key to enable Maya to recognize that she had survived the ordeal of getting lost in the woods. Maya was helped to realize she had evidence that she had survived: For example, simply the fact that she was able to visit the woods, now, as an adult, was a significant piece of survival evidence. On a subsequent visit to the forest, while standing next to the same tree where her traumatic experience began, Maya recounted the many things that had happened in her life since the time she became lost in the woods:

- *graduating elementary, middle, and high school,*
- *graduating college,*
- *meeting Sophie,*
- *getting married,*
- *having children,*
- *and so on.*

That list provided further proof that she had survived.

Eventually, Maya made a plan that would enable her to join her family on the camping trip. She took with her a written timeline of events since her childhood trauma, along with a few objects to remind herself of the fact that she had survived (Key 4). In addition, during the trip, she periodically reminded herself that having family of her own, a partner and children, was very strong evidence that she had, indeed, survived the trauma of being lost in the woods. After that successful camping trip, she and her family were able to enjoy camping together whenever they wanted—at the beach, in the woods, wherever.

The exercises in this chapter, some of which were used by Vanessa with Maya, are designed to help you confirm and celebrate the fact of your own survival. Please take note: You do *not* need to remember the traumatic incident or explore those traumatic memories to recover. Actually, we recommend, at least at this point, that you do *not* focus on your memories at all. The exercises here will focus on what happened since, and what is happening in your life now, to help you recognize that your trauma is over and you have survived. If, at a later date, you decide that you do want to revisit your trauma memories, the process of having first secured your confidence that you survived your ordeal will likely make processing those memories safer and less daunting.

This is a reminder for you to use your Mindful Gauge with the following exercises. You might find the Mindful Gauge to be a handy tool for you. Alternatively, the idea of it might inspire you to an evaluation method of your own design.

First, check with your Mindful Gauge how it feels to read the exercise. If it feels okay to, continue the exercise, and continue to check in. Then check your Mindful Gauge afterwards. Do you feel better or worse? Is this a good resource for you?

CURRENT RESOURCES

What has helped you recover up to now?

What continues to support you in this journey?

A resource is a kind of support that helps you to feel calm and stable. You may find it useful to take stock of the variety of resources that have given you support up to this point. Whether they are practical, like making sure you have locks on your doors, or social, such as knowing your neighbors, the resources that you have and need will be individual to you.

Below, in the box on the left, write the resources you already have. We have given some suggestions to get you started, but feel free to include those or not. It might be useful to use your Mindful Gauge to identify which of our suggestions fit for you, as well as others you want to add. In the box on the right, add resources that you would like to gain or develop.

Practical resources I have (For example: locks on doors and windows, regularly serviced car, cell phone, personal alarm, financial stability)	Practical resources I want to develop
Physical resources I have (For example: exercise class, dancing, gardening, walking, singing, yoga, self-massage)	Physical resources I want to develop

Interpersonal resources I have (For example: knowing my neighbors, being part of a community or activity group, interacting with colleagues, volunteering at a soup kitchen, any and all loved or supportive people *and* animals that are currently in my life)	Interpersonal resources I want to develop
Psychological resources I have (For example: mindfulness, therapy sessions, self-help information, psychological strategies I use to protect myself, even such things as anger or dissociation)	Psychological resources I want to develop
Spiritual resources I have (For example: yoga; meditation; sitting in nature; going to church; watching birds; listening to music; gardening; reading about or listening to inspirational and comforting material about religion, spirituality, or nature)	Spiritual resources I want to develop

IDENTIFY YOUR RAINBOWS, AND BRING THEM WITH YOU

"I've had so many rainbows in my clouds. I had a lot of clouds, but I had so many rainbows. When I go on the stage or teach a class I being everyone who has ever been kind to me with me: Black, white, Asian, Spanish-speaking, Native American, gay, straight, everybody. I say, 'Come on with me. I'm going on the stage. Come with me. I need you now.' ... I don't ever feel I have no help, I've had rainbows in my clouds."
—Maya Angelou

In the previous exercise you took an inventory of the resources that have supported you since the trauma. This exercise focuses specifically on the interpersonal, on the humans and animals in your life that have been a resource.

Maya Angelou (2011) spoke of remembering everyone that had ever been kind to her and holding on to the memory of that person and their kindness, bringing the memory with her in demanding or stressful situations for strength and reassurance.

METHOD

1. In the rainbows below, make a note of the people who have shown you kindness or support, no matter how small. It could be someone who held a door open when you had your hands full, a trusted friend who listened to your problems, a bus driver who let you out at an unscheduled spot, a smiling face in a crowd.

2. Continue adding to these whenever you experience kindness or support, and read through it when your world feels heavy.

3. Choose one of these rainbow memories. Bring to mind everything you can remember about the memory and the person in that memory who showed you kindness. What sensory memory accompanies your memory of that person: visual images, or memories of sounds, smells, tastes, touch, and so on? Some senses may be more or less connected to a particular memory than others.

> **CAVEAT:** No individual is perfect and even the most supportive or kind person can be irritable or even inappropriate at times. For this exercise, choose someone that you feel, on the whole, has been kind to you and focus on the good memories of them. If it is too difficult to focus on the kind memory and you keep remembering an argument you had, choose a different rainbow.

Rainbow memory:	
(nose)	
(lips)	
(ear)	
(hand)	
(eyes)	

4. Now, using your imagination and your Mindful Gauge, notice how it feels to imagine that person standing next to you, offering their kindness, compassion, and encouragement.

    Keep checking in with your Mindful Gauge to notice whether this helps you to feel more calm and stable or not. If *not*, it may be better either to choose another person or perhaps to set this exercise aside for now.

5. If you would like, write or draw encouraging or kind words they might say in the figures below.

Note how you feel and how your system responds to this exercise. Is this something you would like to do again? Sporadically? On a regular basis? If this has been useful for you, perhaps make a plan for where and when it might be useful to use it. You might like to carry a drawing or photograph of, or talisman from, one or more people who have been kind to you, to help remind you of their support. For example, Babette likes to wear earrings and bracelets that were gifts from her rainbows as a reminder of their care.

Basically, the brain has three main parts: the brain stem, the limbic system, and the cortex. The brain stem takes care of basic survival, such as making sure you stay hydrated and nourished. The limbic system is the emotional part of your brain. The cortex is your thinking brain, particularly the part behind your eyes known as the frontal cortex.

One part of the limbic system, the amygdala, takes in information from your senses, associates it with past experience, and tells your body how to respond. If it associates the sensory stimulus as pleasant (like a remembered favorite aroma) the body responds with pleasant sensations. Likewise, if the amygdala associates danger (such as with a loud sound), it activates a fast response, telling the body to fight, flee, or freeze. Another of the structures in the limbic system, the hippocampus, makes sense of events, remembers facts, and works a little like a timekeeper. Part of its job is to keep track of, and log for future reference, the beginning, middle, and end of an event.

Another way to understand what happens when we perceive threat is the Hand Model of the brain, devised by Dan Siegel (2010). He figured out a way to imagine your brain in the palm of your hand. According to Siegel's model, your wrist represents the brain stem; the middle of your hand, including your thumb, represents the limbic system; and your fingers, as they fold over your middle hand and thumb, represent the frontal cortex. See the diagram below for an idea of how this looks.

"LID ON"

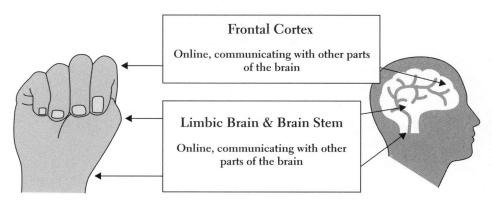

Frontal Cortex

Online, communicating with other parts of the brain

Limbic Brain & Brain Stem

Online, communicating with other parts of the brain

When you are in a calm state the frontal cortex is functional and in communication with the other parts of the brain so you can think clearly to problem-solve, understand, and so on.

"FLIPPED LID"

However, when you get upset, for instance triggered by a reminder of your trauma, you can lose connection to your frontal cortex, your thinking brain, as if you have (as the saying goes) *flipped your lid*. That can also happen when you get anxious, lose your temper, dissolve into tears, and such. The diagram below illustrates the idea of a flipped lid.

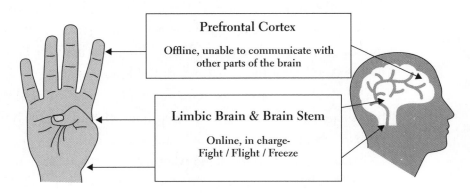

If your nervous system is continuing to react to the danger of your past trauma as if it were still happening or were happening again, it could be a sign that your hippocampus and cortex are overwhelmed and you have flipped your lid. One way to get your lid back on—that is, to be able to think clearly again and perceive your present reality—is to actually, verbally, tell yourself (sometimes over and over again) that the past incident is over, that you survived. (We will also discuss additional ways to calm your nervous system throughout the rest of the book.)

METHOD

Drawing a timeline can provide you with an actual, visual, reinforcement that your life has continued since the ending of your trauma. You can use the example below as an inspiration, but be sure to make your timeline your own. Some people write words, others draw pictures, and another strategy is to use symbols. The important thing is that it should have meaning for you.

Note down events that have happened since the traumatic event ended. You may wish to start with the most recent events first. Include a variety of events: happy and sad times, adventures, and seemingly mundane events. Include new technology, new friends, and new family members that were not around when the trauma occurred.

EXAMPLE

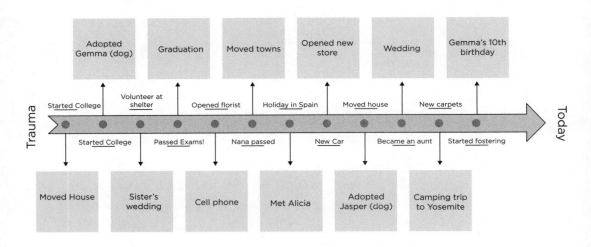

MY TIMELINE

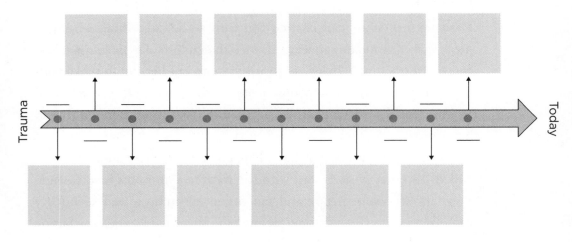

YOUR EPILOGUE

For some people an image like the timeline in the previous exercise is useful, and for others creating an epilogue might be more useful. Or perhaps doing both will be just right for you. If you have done the timeline exercise, then you might use the events listed there to help you write your epilogue, or it could take an entirely different form. Writing is not the only option for your epilogue. Depending on your own tastes, interests, and talents, you might like to draw or sculpt an epilogue or create a collage. What is most important is that it has meaning to you, to reinforce that your trauma is in the past and that you have survived it.

If you are writing, it may be easier to start with today and go backwards in time. Again, choose any and all of the events that come to mind, including happy and sad times, and adventures as well as simpler things, like getting a new refrigerator. New technology can be a great thing to include; as technology changes so quickly through time, the newness of something like a mobile phone or a car is connected to a very distinct moment in time. The technology you have now is likely not to have existed when the trauma happened. Other events that occur at very distinct moments in time include occasions such as the birth of a family member or friend's child, a graduation, or the start of a new job.

Babette has friends who meet regularly to make what they call Soul Collage. They clip pictures from magazines, add photo prints, collect leaves or such from nature, and so on to create something meaningful to themselves for that moment in time. The same idea can absolutely be applied to the idea of an epilogue collage.

Whichever mode you choose to create your epilogue, written or in some other creative mode, make sure that it reminds you and reinforces the truth that your life went on after your trauma ended.

Write your epilogue here:

I SURVIVED!

You are in good company if you feel that your trauma continues or keeps happening, despite actual evidence to the contrary. Many trauma survivors know that whatever it was that happened is over, but they keep reacting as if it were not. In that case, your nervous system may often need reminding that it is over, and that you survived.

Putting your timeline or your written epilogue by your bed to look at or read through in the morning or before you sleep may be a useful reminder. Another strategy could be to write out a few short statements, as below. Keeping copies in different places might help you when you feel overwhelmed or triggered.

METHOD

1. Write short statements to remind you of your survival. Include factual information from your timeline or epilogue.
2. Work out which statements feel most soothing to read. Use your Mindful Gauge to notice your response and help you choose.
3. Make copies of the statements and put them in various places so they will be available to read when you need them. You might choose to put a note in your purse, in coat pockets, stuck to a bathroom mirror, and so on. Put one or more anyplace where they will be easy to find.

Sample statements to inspire you to write your own that will be uniquely suited to you:

- I survived! I know I survived because I am now [52] years old.
- I survived! I know I survived because I now have a cell phone, which was not invented when [the trauma] happened.
- I survived! I know I survived because I am now married to [Jenny].
- I survived! I know I survived because I am now a [grandmother].
- I survived! I know I survived because I am now a [trained and qualified nurse].

Complete some of these sentences for yourself, or create your own. You might find that a different starter for your statements is better. Remember that it is what works for you that counts.

I survived! I know I survived because _____

I survived! I know I survived because _____

I survived! I know I survived because _____

I survived! I know I survived because _____

I survived! I know I survived because _____

I survived! I know I survived because _____

I survived! I know I survived because _____

I survived! I know I survived because _____

I survived! I know I survived because _____

I survived! I know I survived because _____

It might feel good to write out the whole sentences for yourself with additional information that offers proof of your survival:

_____

_____

_____

CELEBRATE AND HONOR YOUR SURVIVAL

Whether or not you want to celebrate your survival, and if you do, how you would go about that, is 100% individual. Celebration is not required to recover from trauma, but for some of you reading this book, it might be a nice idea and a good fit. For ideas, you might take inspiration from one or more fairy tales you are familiar with. They often involve surviving one or more traumas and end with a big celebration, often involving a feast. Depending on your experience, it may be that a celebration of the ending of your trauma was not possible, or you just did not feel like it at the time. Celebrating your survival not only reaffirms to your system that the trauma is over, it also celebrates you. It celebrates your resourcefulness to be here today. The time that has passed since the trauma may have been messy, challenging, and distressing, but the fact remains that you survived.

There are many ways to celebrate following a dark time in life. Injured soldiers are awarded a Purple Heart. Similarly, as she shared in her book 8 *Keys to Safe Trauma Recovery* (to which this workbook is a companion), author Babette searched for and then found and bought a heart brooch to remind her that she survived a childhood trauma. Author Vanessa planted a tree years after her trauma. Each spring the leaves and blossoms reassure her that life and growth continue, and remind her of her connection to and belonging in nature.

Many Indigenous communities historically have performed, and often still do, rituals that included the elements, such as fire and water, after a battle, war, flood, or other period of hardship.

For you, for example, a fire ritual could involve writing the title of the trauma onto a piece of paper that is then burned in a fireplace or firepit. Another possibility might be to dance or sing around an actual or imagined campfire. A water ritual might involve dropping a pebble into a lake or ocean. Another idea could be to make a miniature boat that you allow to float away.

Another idea, for some, would be to take a day's holiday, once or even around the same time each year, spending such a day engaging in enjoyable activities they might not otherwise make time for. Consider whether you would like to get creative and sculpt, draw, or paint a celebration of your survival. Then you could decide where you would like to keep or display it so you could see it regularly or, alternatively, to destroy your creation so you would no longer be reminded.

Celebrations can be private or shared with others. It is up to you to choose whether you wish to celebrate your survival alone or with others. Use your Mindful Gauge to help you choose what, if anything, you want to do, and who, if anyone, you want to share your special event or artwork with. Prioritize those who would be the most supportive and glad for your celebration.

METHOD

1. Notice whether you want to celebrate in multiple ways or to plan a single way to honor your survival.
2. Use your Mindful Gauge to work out what is right for you, step by step.
3. Notice whether it is something you would like to do once, or whether you would like to make it into a ritual, a way of recognizing and honoring your survival every day, week, month, or year.
4. If you would like to share the experience, use your Mindful Gauge to help you choose who would be most appropriate. (Caveat: It is probably *not* a good idea to share the details of your trauma story with your celebration attendees.)

Check any of these suggestions that appeal to you and then use the space below to plan. The suggestions below do not include all possibilities. Feel free to add more possibilities for celebrating your survival that you or others think of.

☐ Make or buy a badge or brooch of honor

☐ Select, make, or purchase an item of jewelry that signifies your survival

☐ Give a special gift to yourself

- ☐ Plan a feast or party with people in your life who are important to you

- ☐ Plant a tree or flower bush

- ☐ Create a Celebration of your survival with singing and dancing

- ☐ Create a ritual with water, fire, or other natural elements

- ☐ Plan a Celebration of Survival Holiday

- ☐ Make a painting, sculpture, or collage to represent and celebrate your survival

- ☐ Create a bucket list and check off items from it

- ☐ Plan a day enjoying activities that bring you joy

- ☐ Paint, draw, or use creative writing to express your survival

Plan to celebrate my survival:

Key Review

Did you remember to use your Mindful Gauge to evaluate the exercises in this chapter? If not, was that by choice or because you forgot?

	Did this exercise help, or make you feel worse?	If it helped, what reaction did you have that told you it helped? (For example, felt calmer or stronger or more present.)
Current Resources		
Identify Your Rainbows, and Bring Them With You		
Timeline		
Your Epilogue		
I Survived!		
Celebrate and Honor Your Survival		

If you forgot, consider whether you want to go back and do that.
Once you have completed an exercise you may wish to jot down your response and its effectiveness for you in the table.

If it helped, could it be adapted to help more? How?	If it helped, when do you plan to use it?	If it did not help, could you change or adapt it to better suit you? How?

KEY 3 REMEMBERING IS NOT REQUIRED

> We feel safe in our bodies when we know that as stress
> (internal or external) pushes us out of the comfort
> zone, we can find our way back through a variety of
> personally reliable techniques for regaining balance.
>
> —BONNIE BADENOCH, *Being a Brain-Wise Therapist*

A common misbelief, held by therapists *and* clients alike, about trauma therapy is that it is essential for traumatic memories to be explored and processed in order for recovery to take place. There is no research that supports this being true. Consider this: Trauma therapy is a relatively new treatment option in the history of humankind. For the thousands and thousands of years before its invention, the majority of humans nonetheless recovered from trauma. If not, we would not be here. Of course, that is not to say that for some people, exploring their trauma might be very beneficial. However, for many, revisiting memories of traumatic incidents is very destabilizing and worsens symptoms. What we want to underscore here is: **You have, and should always have, the option to *not* talk about or remember your trauma.** And you should *never* be forced to remember trauma as part of a course of therapy. A good reason not to remember is if you simply do not want to. In addition, we can assure you that you can, indeed, recover from your trauma without remembering, just as your ancestors did. And if you do want to remember your trauma, when you are stable enough to manage that in a way that helps you to heal, we support that also.

Below we will give guidelines for when or whether trauma-memory processing would be a good idea. But for now, suffice it to say that it is not a good idea for the main goal of trauma therapy to be revisiting memories. Instead, it should always be to *improve your quality of life.* This includes ensuring you are able to be in control of any symptoms you have (even stopping flashbacks, which will be discussed in the next chapter), to function on a daily basis (for example, being able to maintain healthy relationships), to follow through with your usual responsibilities (at work, home, or school), and to take part in activities you enjoy.

Toward the end of the 19th century Dr. Pierre Janet (1889/1973) developed a three-phased approach to trauma treatment that is still very much respected and practiced today by many prominent trauma specialists. It is a structure that can be used with any trauma treatment modality and contains lots of common sense. The first phase focuses on developing safety and stabilization; the second involves processing the trauma memories; the third addresses integration. The term "processing trauma" means retelling or reflecting on the traumatic story in the hopes of gaining insight or desensitizing to the memory. The third phase focuses on integration of what is learned from Phases 1 and 2. That may include gaining a new perspective, learning new tools or strengthening ones you have, and using insights to improve your daily life.

This phased method was initially suggested as a linear approach, with the phases being tackled in order, one after the other, first, second, third. However, it is our recommendation to address Phase 3 simultaneously with Phases 1 and 2 so that you can integrate what you are learning and apply it to better your daily life every step of the way. For example, that is a part of our goal in giving you a Key Review at the end of each chapter of this book.

Some of our clients have reported friends, family, and therapists telling them that if they do not remember and recount the intricate details of their trauma story then they are avoiding it, or might never be able to recover. We could not disagree more. People recover from trauma all the time without reviewing their memories and, as mentioned above, have been doing so throughout time. We are not suggesting that you push down your memories or try to forget what happened to you, but we believe that any exploration of trauma memories should be a choice based on what is best for you at a particular point in time. Any decision for processing memories should be held off until it can be done in a healing and integrating way.

For example, if you were planning to safely rappel down a mountainside, you would not just grab a rope and leap. Before you started, you would check that the rope was anchored properly and securely and was strong enough to support you, and that you had the skills and support of others necessary to be able to rappel down the mountain. Of course, we are also not suggesting that by working through Phase 1 you will never be triggered or overwhelmed again. Rather, we are suggesting that when that happens, you will gain the ability to reliably and consistently calm yourself, manage your symptoms (including dissociation), and connect to the present.

Having achieved a feeling of reliable safety and stabilization (Phase 1) and integrated the tools that help them maintain that in their daily life (Phase 3), many of our clients, and those of Babette's trainees, report such an improvement in their quality of life that they do not feel the need to process their trauma memories (Phase 2).

During most of Babette's professional training programs, which are attended primarily by professional psychotherapists and counselors, she conducts an informal poll regarding the attendees' own personal experience in processing trauma memories. She asks how many of those attending have trauma in their backgrounds that they have not processed while they nonetheless have a basically good quality of life. Generally, two thirds to four fifths of the group's attendees raise their hand. This means that most therapists (at least those attending Babette's trainings, but likely others as well) have *not* processed all of their traumas and yet maintain a good quality of life. Nonetheless, many still insist that their clients process their trauma memories. That contradiction is an interesting one for the professionals to grapple with.

"What If I Do Not Remember at All?"

It is common for some of those who encounter trauma to experience confusion about the incident or complete or partial loss of their memory of it. Why someone does not remember trauma can have to do with the complexities of the mind and brain or can simply be due to their age or degree of consciousness/unconsciousness at the time of the experience. The good news is that anyone can recover from trauma and have a good quality of life even if they do not remember their trauma (and people do, all the time).

It is also important to note that it is never a good idea to try to remember all, or parts, of a trauma that you have forgotten or during which you were not conscious. Attempting to reveal a forgotten or suspected memory often results in a worsening of symptoms, creates *false memories*, and contributes to overall confusion about what did or did not happen. In such instances, it is better to focus on improving your current quality of life, which includes taking charge of your symptoms, rather than trying to seek out a forgotten or unknown past.

This may be a good place to mention a rather controversial point of view: From our clinical experience, we have come to believe that, as a profession, we have given much too much attention to the past. As said previously, of course there can be benefit in this for some, but definitely not all, people. However, one of the few facts that you can rely on is that *you cannot change the past.* Nonetheless, there is much you can do to improve your present life and take steps and lay foundations for a better future. It is for that reason that in these pages we will be focusing on exactly that.

What Can Help

The exercises in this chapter focus on how to improve your quality of life without having to revisit trauma memories. That includes identifying which of Pierre Janet's phases makes the most sense for you, on the whole, *right now*, helping you to gain and strengthen tools to increase your emotional stability, and to learn strategies for integrating those into your daily life.

Phases 1 and 3 are appropriate for everyone. For some they will provide the route to trauma recovery with*out* ever approaching Phase 2. For others, Phases 1 and 3 will be the foundation for work in Phase 2.

One important thing to note is that every exercise in this book is part of either Phase 1 or Phase 3; we have not included any exercises that offer processing of trauma memories. We hope that the exercises in this book will bring you more stability, rather than overwhelm you; however, every individual has their own capacities. We strongly encourage you to STOP if you feel less stable doing any of the exercises. If you decide that working in Phase 2 is appropriate for you now or in the future, we would recommend engaging a trauma therapist to accompany you and first laying a secure foundation in Phase 1.

As with all the exercises in this book, we encourage you to read through them first and use your Mindful Gauge (from Key 1) to help you decide which ones seem good for you to try. Continue to use your Mindful Gauge as you do each exercise to stay aware of your reactions.

This is a reminder for you to use your Mindful Gauge with the following exercises. You might find the Mindful Gauge to be a handy tool for you. Alternatively, the idea of it might inspire you to an evaluation method of your own design.

First, check with your Mindful Gauge how it feels to read the exercise. If it feels okay, then continue the exercise, and continue to check in. Make sure to check your Mindful Gauge afterwards. Do you feel better or worse for having tried the exercise? Is it a good resource for you?

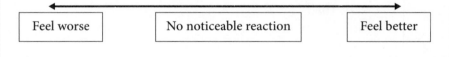

| Feel worse | No noticeable reaction | Feel better |

WHICH PHASE IS MOST USEFUL FOR YOU RIGHT NOW?

Deciding which phase is most helpful for you now will be a useful place to start when deciding where to head next in your trauma-recovery journey. As mentioned, all of the exercises in this book focus on Phases 1 and 3. Nonetheless, if you decide that Phase 2 is something that you want to explore, and you feel that you are stable enough to begin that, then the exercises in this section may help you build or increase the stabilization that you will need when processing your memories.

THE THREE (NONLINEAR) PHASES

Phase 1:

Establish reliable safety and stabilization in your life

Phase 2:

Processing trauma memories

Phase 3:

Integration of Phase 1 and 2 in daily life

ASSESS YOUR SAFETY AND STABILITY

Phase 1 and Phase 3 are the quickest route to stabilization, safety, and trauma recovery.

Read through the statements written in the boxes below and notice whether they are true to your current circumstances. Any that you answer "no" to are good candidates to be among your initial tasks for your trauma recovery.

I have the basics for everyday life: food, shelter, clothing, and healthy companionship (network).

I can control my emotions. If I have a flashback or feel anxious, panicked, or overwhelmed, I can calm myself and anchor my attention in the here and now.

(Find resources to help with this in the next chapter, Key 4.)

I can manage a normal day of activities and responsibilities.

(Based on what is normal in your family or culture: worker, student, parent, or other.)

Read through the statements written in the boxes below. Notice which is most applicable to you and whether it is true to your current circumstances of safety.

If you had an accident, the cause has been rectified (e.g., the car has been fixed, the wobbly step is repaired).

If you are a refugee, you have legal right to remain in a safe enough country.

If you were a victim of violence, you are physically healed.

The perpetrator is dead or incarcerated or you are otherwise adequately protected.

If you were a victim of domestic abuse, you are no longer living with the abuser, or they have stopped being abusive and you are both having successful counseling and support.

If you were abused as a child, you no longer have a relationship with, or live with or near to the abuser.

You are currently not continuing to live under the threat of trauma, including abuse, war, life-threatening illness, and so on.

This is not, by any means, an exhaustive list. Though none of these may apply to you, it is the principle that is important: Are you still in danger of the same trauma you are attempting to recover from, or any other situation that includes trauma? If you are, you may need to assess and plan how to make yourself safe. That might mean getting into contact with local services, charities, or trusted friends to help. The Safety and Stability Wish List exercise, below, may also help you to identify your needs.

Take note: For you, the basis of Phase 1 work may be to get yourself into a safe living situation. However, never attempt Phase 2 work unless and until you are living, on a daily basis, in safety.

TRAUMA TYPES

An important consideration when weighing up whether to explore trauma memories is your trauma type. Reading the following trauma types, notice which most applies to you.

Resolved Trauma

You have experienced trauma in the past but it does not affect your daily life or your nervous system. If you have a good quality of life and past trauma does not negatively affect you, then you may want to consider why you would upset the apple cart by processing trauma memories.

Trauma is often healed without trauma therapy, usually through good contact and support from one or more close relation-ships. It is absolutely possible that you have healed without the need for formal intervention.

Single Unresolved Trauma

You have only experienced a single traumatic event that has now ended (see Key 2) but continues to affect you negatively. Or you have experienced more than one, but the other(s) are resolved.

If you are currently stable and safe and are able to maintain those feelings of stability and safety when reflecting on the past, then exploring your trauma memories may be appropriate for you—if you choose to.

Trauma Types

Multiple Unresolved Trauma, Stable

You experienced multiple, separate traumatic incidents. When you reflect on the past you can coherently differentiate between the separate traumas without jumbling them up.

Once you feel safe and stable enough and are able to calm yourself when thinking of the past, you may wish to explore Phase 2, one incident at a time, if that is something you want to do and feel that you would likely benefit from.

Multiple Unresolved Trauma, Unstable

You have experienced more than one traumatic event. When you reflect on the past it is difficult to separate them, or details from different incidents leak into or trigger others.

At this time, we would not recommend Phase 2 work for you.

These exercises will help you decide whether you *want* to process memories and deal with pressure from others if you do not.

Whether to process your trauma memories is not a decision to be taken lightly. Some people never want to revisit their trauma memories, whether they believe it would make a difference to their life or not. Many choose not to, knowing that their quality of life can be improved and that they can recover from trauma without processing their trauma memories. If you answered yes to each of the questions in the Assess Your Safety and Stability exercise, that does not mean that exploring the trauma is something you *should* do, or that you have to do. Some are very relieved to know they can recover from trauma without having to remember. Are you? Whichever, if you do not want to remember what happened to you, you should never be forced to. Ever.

Both Babette and Vanessa have experienced therapists pushing them to remember trauma when they did not want to. We have also both known many clients whose friends, family, and therapists have warned them that they could recover only if they "stop avoiding the past," or that they "must face it head on" and such. Actually, this is an outdated view and is simply not true.

In reality, most people recover from trauma without any trauma therapy at all. Resources of all sorts have helped humans recover from trauma for all of time. These include, but are not limited to, good contact and support from both humans and animals, useful work, faith of some sort, and relationship to nature. That is not to say that trauma therapy is a bad thing. Remember, Babette and Vanessa are both trauma therapists. What is most important is that you find what you most need to recover, whether that includes therapy or not. This may be a good place to mention that trauma therapy should not be only about processing trauma memories. Trauma therapists should also be making sure their clients are reliably stable and safe before attempting Phase 2 work. It is also important that therapists are able and willing to help clients to recover from trauma without working in Phase 2; otherwise they could inadvertently push into processing trauma those clients who either are not equipped to do so or do not want to.

Of course, the likely reason that you are reading this book is that so far your resources have not been adequate to enable your recovery. Just do not lose faith in the possibility that they can, and that you can add to and strengthen your resources for exactly that purpose and to better your quality of life in general. Knowing that resources can help you recover gives you more options, whether or not you decide to process your memories. In the next chapter, Key 4, there will be a lengthy discussion of resources and exercises to help you to expand your supply of them.

The first part of this next exercise is to help you decide whether you want to process your trauma memories or not. Using the guidelines for assessing stability, above, notice (or remember) how focusing on the past affects you. Does it cause you to become less able to manage tasks in your present daily life or to withdraw from your support network? If focusing on the past decreases your ability to manage and enjoy your life here and now, then it may not be something that will benefit you, at least not right now. If you assess that you are stable enough to process trauma memories, then the Pros and Cons exercise that follows this one may help you decide whether it is something that you want to do.

Use your Mindful Gauge to check whether it is something you *want* to do, and consider why and how it will be of benefit to you.

PROS AND CONS

After assessing your current safety, stability, and trauma type, you may feel that Phase 2 might be a sensible option for you. What more do you need to make your decision?

METHOD

Use the chart below to list the pros and cons of exploring your trauma memories to help you make a decision. You may also wish to determine their importance by using your Mindful Gauge.

Pros	Cons

If you decide that you are safe and stable enough, that your trauma type is appropriate, and that your pros outweigh your cons, then your next step is planning a safe way to explore your trauma memories. We recommend that you do this with a therapist, that you use your Mindful Gauge and, like Goldilocks in Key 1, you allow yourself to be picky in choosing the therapist who is just right for you. Remember that you can change your mind at any point. Deciding this today does not mean that it has to be your decision tomorrow.

If you decide you do not want to process your trauma memories, this next exercise applies to you. When you feel that people are pushing you to explore your trauma memories, particularly those who appear to have authority, such as therapists, it can be difficult to say no. This exercise provides you with options you can use to hold your boundaries when you feel pressured. When Babette was living in Denmark and going to therapy as part of being a student in the Bodynamic Analysis training, there came a time when she needed to assert her own authority with her therapist. Though she was very nervous to do it, and it took a little time to work up her courage, eventually she was able to tell her therapist that she would no longer be pushed into doing something they had not discussed and agreed on together, and that if the result of saying no to something meant that the therapy took longer, so be it. Gratefully, her therapist was comfortable with agreeing to Babette's terms and they continued to work together with mutual respect. It was definitely not easy to do. But in the end, Babette was glad she had dared. Not only did it make the therapy safer and more productive for her, she also gained greater confidence in her ability to guide her own therapy as well as her own life.

METHOD

1. Read through the statements below.
2. Use your Mindful Gauge to notice how each statement affects you.
3. Using your own language, or a mixture of the statements below together with your own words, write out one or more statements to use when you feel pressured to process your trauma memories.

4. Read these, or your own statements, aloud a few times each and check in with your Mindful Gauge to see if you want to make any changes. Notice whether you want to make any gestures with your hands, your body, or your face to emphasize what you are saying. You may or may not decide to use any gestures if you are actually confronted, but when practicing the statements, they might help you feel stronger. You might even try it in front of a mirror or with a trusted friend.

5. Write your statements and keep them close at hand. You can write on paper to keep in your pocket or on a note app in your phone. You may wish to read it a few times before a situation where you might expect to be challenged.

6. If it feels too difficult to tell the person pushing you, you may wish to simply hand them the note to read. If you want extra backup, you could show them the chapter of this book.

Here are some examples to try or to edit into what feels comfortable to you.

I know we talked about that last week, but this week I do not want to.

I have a right to choose my own recovery path.

I know best what is right for me.

I can see that our opinions on this are different. I might be wrong, but this way makes more sense for me.

When I tried what you asked, I felt worse.

Now, write one or more statements that you might use if you feel pressured into talking about your trauma. Read through them and choose which feels most right for you.

Additional Tools for Stabilization

You will find tools that help with stabilization throughout this book—for example, being present through mindfulness (Key 1); identifying and employing resources (Key 2); grounding to help manage flashbacks (Key 4). Key 7 explores more physical and body-oriented ways to stabilize. Below are some additional tools specifically related to achieving and maintaining stability to improve your quality of life.

SAFETY AND STABILITY WISH LIST

In Key 2 we explored the resources that you already have that have helped you to cope since the trauma. As you were making those lists, you may have noticed some gaps, where your needs for safety and stability are not yet adequately met. Consider, for example, would you like better locks on your doors, or to move to a different neighborhood? How about increasing physical activity or learning how to say no?

METHOD

Using the chart below, make a note of the things that currently help you feel safe and resources that could improve your sense of safety and stability. It is fine if there is crossover with any of the resources that you identified in Key 2.

Functional resources to help me feel safer and more stable (For example: to have adequate locks on my windows and doors, to have a steady income, to find work during the daytime rather than at night)	Physical resources to help me feel safer and more stable (For example: to feel strong in my body, to attend a trauma-aware self-defense class)

Interpersonal resources to help me feel safer and more stable (For example: to live near a trusted friend, to feel part of a community, to know my neighbors, to get a cat to keep me company)	Spiritual resources to help me feel safer and more stable (For example: to take time out of my day to sit in nature, to find a place of worship where I feel calm)
Psychological resources to help me feel safer and more stable (For example: to embrace my talent for dissociation, to get better at knowing when I am angry and at saying no)	Other resources to help me feel safer and more stable (For example: to identify the music and films that soothe me)

Notice which ones you have available now and which you need more time to develop. It may be useful to refer to Key 6 to help you break down bigger changes into smaller, more manageable steps.

ROUTINES AND RITUALS

Many people feel more stable when they have a set and reliable routine in their daily life. That makes sense, as humans are creatures of habit who tend to feel safer when they know what to expect.

In contrast, a variety of memes and platitudes found on social media encourage people to "step out of your comfort zone," declaring this is "where the magic happens," implying that discomfort is good for everyone. However, that is not necessarily true. Each person is different. The point is to know what suits *you*. You may decide to keep to your comfort zone or to challenge yourself. However, it does not need to be an all-or-nothing choice. The nervous excitement you might feel trying something new can be tempered by employing tools such as grounding and stabilization. Routines can also help. For example, many professional rock climbers prefer to *not* feel an adrenaline rush when doing high-risk climbs. Many need exactly the opposite, a sense of total calm, so that they can think clearly. To ensure that, a good number of climbers utilize rituals and routines, such as starting each climb at a certain time of day, or checking their equipment in a particular order, or keeping a talisman or two in their pocket. Though circumstances, such as weather, may change during a climb, the climber's rituals help them to feel control wherever they can. That, in turn, calms their nervous system, ensuring that, should bad weather arrive, they are well prepared to deal with it.

Inserting routines into everyday life might help reduce any stress that comes with sudden or unwelcome change. Routine provides a stable platform from which to make considered and meaningful change when the opportunity for change arises.

Consider the things you are able to do at set times each day, week, or month. These might include mealtimes, exercising, calling or meeting friends, walking the dog, resting, waking up, and going to bed. That does not mean that every waking minute should be scheduled. Like everything else, this is individual. Identifying which activities are most suitable for routines in *your* life is one of the Keys to making it work for you.

METHOD

1. Read through the daily activities listed, checking the ones you recognize and adding any others that apply to you.

2. In the space next to the activity, write down a time when you wish to do or already do this activity.

3. You may choose to add these times to your cell-phone calendar so that you get reminders, or to your wall calendar, to help you keep the habit.

4. If you are planning a vacation or break, consider which routines you will be able to keep and which you will modify. Often, during and following the holidays, people experience destabilization caused by the lack of or break in routine. For example, you may wish to wake later during a restful holiday. In that case, would it be better to wake at that later time each day during the break, or would you rather just not set an alarm? Or you may decide to eat at different times during the holidays, but keep some of your other routines the same.

Daily Routine

☐ Wake up	_____ a.m./p.m.	☐ Eat lunch	_____ a.m./p.m.
☐ Eat breakfast	_____ a.m./p.m.	☐ Leave work	_____ a.m./p.m.
☐ Feed pets	_____ a.m./p.m.	☐ Pick up children	_____ a.m./p.m.
☐ Walk dogs	_____ a.m./p.m.	☐ Activity that brings you joy	_____ a.m./p.m.
☐ Take children to school	_____ a.m./p.m.	☐ Eat dinner	_____ a.m./p.m.
☐ Exercise	_____ a.m./p.m.	☐ Shower/bath	_____ a.m./p.m.
☐ Go to work	_____ a.m./p.m.	☐ Go to bed	_____ a.m./p.m.

Other Daily Activities

_____ at _____ a.m./p.m.   _____ at _____ a.m./p.m.

_____ at _____ a.m./p.m.   _____ at _____ a.m./p.m.

_____ at _____ a.m./p.m.   _____ at _____ a.m./p.m.

_____ at _____ a.m./p.m.   _____ at _____ a.m./p.m.

_____ at _____ a.m./p.m.   _____ at _____ a.m./p.m.

Weekly Rituals

Call _____ (friend/family) on _____ (day) at _____ a.m./p.m.

Meet _____ (friend/family) on _____ (day) at _____ a.m./p.m.

Go to _____ (exercise class/group/café) on _____ (day)

at _____ a.m./p.m.

Other Weekly Rituals

_____ on _____ (day) at _____ a.m./p.m.

_____ on _____ (day) at _____ a.m./p.m.

_____ on _____ (day) at _____ a.m./p.m.

_____ on _____ (day) at _____ a.m./p.m.

_____ on _____ (day) at _____ a.m./p.m.

STABILIZATION BREAKS

Trauma can shake you to your core. As with a shaken-up bottle of soda (mineral water, cola, and the like), opening the bottle all at once can make a mess. Working on Phase 2 before becoming reliably safe and stable in your life can be like opening a pressurized soda bottle all at once. To safely open it, you must *slowly* unscrew the cap, letting out a little bit of fizz at a time: Open a little, close, open a little, close. Relieving the pressure slowly is the key to opening those bottles without any mess. It is actually a good exercise in pressure control to try with a bottle of soda yourself. Practice being in control of the fizz by very slowly releasing the pressure so you can open the bottle without getting the soda all over you and the floor.

Many people with PTSD experience something similar in daily life. Pressure builds throughout the day, a combination of stressors and triggers acting as reminders of past trauma and shaking you up, until finally you explode and flip your lid. The explosion could take the form of an anxiety attack, an angry outburst, or a full-blown flashback.

Planning calming breaks throughout your day to do stabilizing activities can help to let off some pressure and maintain equilibrium. The old wisdom, that prevention is better than cure, applies here.

METHOD

1. Read through the Key Reviews of the chapters of this book that you have already completed. Notice the exercises that helped you find a sense of calm and stability. You might already have some from elsewhere too (other books, classes, therapy, your own invention)— great! Add those to your list.

2. Set specific times throughout your day to have stabilizing breaks. As we discussed above, scheduling the same time each day will help to set a habit that also offers stability.

3. Set an alarm on your cell phone or your watch, or add "SB" (stabilization break) to your desk or computer calendar to remind you to take the breaks. You may be tempted to skip this step, but when you most need the stabilization break is likely to be when you forget it.

4. Plan ahead. Decide beforehand, using your Mindful Gauge, three options of stabilizing activities to do. You will probably do only one at each break, but having clear options gives you structure as well as choice. Use your Mindful Gauge to help you choose which of the three is best for that moment.

DAILY STABILIZATION BREAKS SCHEDULE

	Time	Three stabilizing options (so you can choose)		
Morning				
Lunch				
Mid-afternoon				
Evening				

SAFE-PLACE MEMORY

Memories of past trauma can influence your feelings in the present; that is why flashbacks feel so powerful. However, pleasant memories can also influence how you feel now; sometimes they can even be so powerful that they can antidote a flashback. This exercise is intended to help you identify one or more memories that might have such potential. Choose a memory of a place where you felt safe, supported, treated kindly, or such.

This exercise must be done with an *actual* memory of a real place where you felt safe. It could have been for any period of time: a fleeting moment, an hour or two, a full day, weeks, or even longer. Aim to keep your attention on a specific time slot when you felt most safe there, even if it was just for a moment. Start small.

Do not look for a place where you felt perfectly safe. As with most things in life, nothing is 100%. Look, instead, for "good enough" safe. It is possible that right now you might not remember a place where you felt safe. If so, skip this exercise for now and come back to it at a later time.

METHOD

Take a moment to remember a place and time you felt safe. It might be a long time ago, or more recent. If you have a photograph of that place or there are pictures of the place on the internet, then you might like to look at one as you do this exercise.

1. As you recall that memory, use your Mindful Gauge to notice your response. If at any time you start to feel less calm, stop.
2. Focusing on that memory, jot down what you remember seeing, smelling, tasting, hearing, and touching when you were in that safe place. And then notice how your remembering affects these same features in the present moment.

	Remembered sensations	Right-now sensations
👀 See		
👃 Smell		
👄 Taste		
👂 Hear		
✋ Touch/Feel		

3. What does safety *feel* like to you?

As you remember that safe place, you may notice emotions, sensations, thoughts, images, and moods arise. Make a note of them in the table below. It may be easier to just focus on one of the rows—choose either body sensations, thoughts, mind's images, or emotions. You may wish to note from other sections whether it feels right for you.

Body sen-sations	Relaxed chest	Soft belly	Lengthened spine	Sighing	Steady heartbeat
	Soft muscles	Soft eyes	Warm hands	Steady breathing	

Thoughts, poems, sayings, analogies, songs	I can . . .	I love the . . .	I know that . . .	This reminds me of . . .	I am . . .
	I am glad it is . . .				
Emotions	Cozy	Cheerful	Sleepy	Satisfied	Excited
	Energized	Peaceful			

Mind's images—memories of smells, tastes, sounds, sights, inner impulses	*Draw or describe any image(s) in your mind as you remember that safe place.*
Any other noticeable reactions	

4. Keep checking in with your Mindful Gauge. Write a description of that safe memory, including all the sensory memories from the table above. You may prefer to draw or paint or sculpt it. You may wish to do all of these, to really embed that memory and feeling of safety. Notice what is right for you.

5. If this exercise helped to elicit a feeling of safety, you might choose to make reminders of your safe place to help you to connect with that feeling either during a planned stabilization break or if you feel overwhelmed. You could choose to carry a photograph, drawing, or painting of your safe place in your purse, or have it put in a key chain, printed on the back of a cell-phone cover, or printed onto a cushion or a mug.

WHAT DOES FEELING SAFE AND STABLE MEAN TO YOU?

If you have completed the previous exercise, you may have established how safety feels to you. This can be helpful in recognizing that feeling of safety in the future. Following trauma, people naturally focus more on negative feelings and experiences. This seems like common sense, evolutionarily. If someone was bitten by a snake and narrowly survived, looking out for snakes in future would be a sensible thing to do. The human race would not have survived without a little anxiety and vigilance.

However, experiencing trauma symptoms over an extended period of time can sometimes cause a diminished ability to identify and notice feelings of safety and stability; it is possible to forget what calm and safe feel like.

Kara could not remember when they last felt safe and stable. They described their days as filled with fear since the traumatic event. They wanted to increase levels of safety and stability but had not really taken stock of what they already did in their life that cultivated those feelings. Taking time to identify what safety felt like to them meant that they were more able to notice it and what had caused it so that they could incorporate more of those activities, places, and people into their day.

METHOD

Read the questions below and write or draw your answers using your Mindful Gauge to help you work out what feels right for you.

1. What does it mean, to me, to be safe?

2. What does it mean, to me, to feel stable?

3. How do my body and mind let me know that I am safe?
   You may wish to refer back to the previous exercise, if
   appropriate.

4. When do you feel most safe in your life now? Use your Mindful
   Gauge to assess how safe you feel during the next week. Complete
   the chart to identify what helps and what hinders feeling safe.
   In the day and time boxes, note what you were doing, who you
   were with, and where you were.
   Also, note your feelings of safety and stability from 10 (*I feel
   least safe*) to 1 (*I feel very safe*).

Example: Kara's Safe and Stable weekly assessment

		Monday	Tuesday	Wednesday
Morn-ing	Activity	Eat breakfast	Eat breakfast	Eat breakfast
	People	Sheila	Sheila	Sheila
	Setting	Home	Coffee shop	Home
	Safety level 1–10	2	5	2
Lunch-time	Activity	Travel to work	Travel to work	Travel to work
	People	Alone/other transport users	Alone/other transport users	Alone
	Setting	Bus	Bus	Bicycle
	Safety level 1–10	7	8	3
After-noon	Activity	Walk the dogs	Walk dogs	Walk dogs
	People	Alone/dogs	Thomas and dogs	Alone/dogs
	Setting	Park	Park	Park
	Safety level 1–10	5	2	6

This excerpt seems to suggest that Kara feels safest at home with Sheila, and walking the dogs with Thomas. Seeing that so clearly, they might be inspired to arrange more dog walks with Thomas in the future. They seem to feel significantly safer riding their bike to work than taking public transport. This might be something that they would do more often now that they are aware of it.

		Monday	Tuesday	Wednesday
Morning	Activity			
	People			
	Setting			
	Safety level 1–10			
Lunch-time	Activity			
	People			
	Setting			
	Safety level 1–10			
After-noon	Activity			
	People			
	Setting			
	Safety level 1–10			
Evening	Activity			
	People			
	Setting			
	Safety level 1–10			

Thursday	Friday	Saturday	Sunday

Evaluate and note down any important insights or conclusions from your table above. Notice which activities, people, places help you feel safest and where you could increase time spent in circumstances where you feel safest.

MAKE A DATE WITH CALM

What activities could you make a daily or weekly date with yourself to do that would bring you a feeling of calm? Notice which small activities could bring a better quality of life if added to your day-to-day routine.

You may have already identified some calming activities in the last exercise. In the space below, take some time to consider any additional strategies, no matter how tiny or large, you could implement in your daily life to give you reminders or oases of calm. Here are some examples that may inspire you to broaden the scope of your choices:

- Vanessa takes time out of each day to sit in a favorite spot in nature to notice the daily and seasonal changes in the leaves, flowers, and creatures around her. She might paint or doodle what she finds, or she may simply allow mindful awareness of her senses to take a needed break by anchoring in the present moment.
- Babette likes to watch the free ArmchairTourist channel on her Roku player, enjoying the shifting 90-second videos from around the world.
- A therapist colleague of ours buys herself fresh flowers each week to brighten her home.
- Other friends feel calm doing jigsaw puzzles, gardening, baking bread, taking short and long walks, helping a neighbor, and so on.

The point is that the possibilities are endless and very individual.

METHOD

1. Read through the suggestions below and use your Mindful Gauge to notice your response to each. Mark the ones that appeal to you.
2. Add all others that you would like to try, or already do. It might help to think of things that you enjoyed when you were a child.
3. Then, one at a time, use your Mindful Gauge to choose which you would like to try incorporating into your coming week. You may already know or, like Goldilocks, who we mentioned in Key 1, you may wish to try different strategies to help you figure out what is just right for you now.

4. Return to this exercise regularly so that you have the opportunity to choose different activities to try, gradually growing the supplies in your calming toolbox.

INCREASING FOCUS AND ATTENTION

Have you noticed whether you are easily distracted? Those with PTSD often have trouble concentrating, holding their attention on one thing. Constantly shifting attention can sabotage your attempts to focus or feel calm as well as to accomplish most kinds of work and other tasks. Strengthening your ability to focus on, and stick with, one thing at a time will help with that.

Engaging in activities that hold your attention, particularly those that use hand-eye coordination, can be a powerful tool for keeping your focus on that one thing. That, in turn, can help you to feel calm and find stability when you feel overwhelmed. When Babette was recovering from PTSD in the 1980s she learned to play more than a dozen different games of solitaire, even reading several books on the solo card games to expand her playing options. She found that playing with the cards, handling them, and concentrating on the strategy would always help her calm down.

METHOD

1. Use your Mindful Gauge to choose pleasant activities that you know from past experience or want to try.
2. Include any activities in your list that have held your concentration in the past.
3. Choose one or two of these activities to try over the next couple of days.
4. Check in with your Mindful Gauge before and after each activity to evaluate whether it is helpful to your concentration and calm.
5. Make a note of ones that work well so that you can call on them to help you stabilize in the future.

6. Below you can keep a running list of helpful focusing activities to refer to.

Activities that worked best at helping me focus and feel calm:

CHOOSING THE RIGHT CHAIR

This exercise is reminiscent of the Goldilocks story mentioned in Key 1. Being aware of seemingly small things can affect your feeling of safety and stability and can have a huge effect on your ability to feel calm and enjoy a good quality of life. This exercise about choosing where to sit may or may not be relevant for you. However, you can use the same principles and adapt the instructions to apply to other situations, small or big. Maybe for you it will be important to pay attention to where and how you stand when speaking with someone, or the distance you sit from your television, or it might include the volume on your phone for conversation or music, or the placement of your bed or other furniture in your home, and so on.

Whenever Alisha goes into a café, she looks for a table near the front so that she feels she can leave quickly if she chooses to, and finds a chair where she has her back to a wall and faces the door. From this position she can see most of the room, is unlikely to be startled by someone behind her, and has a good view of people coming and going. From experimenting with sitting in different places and using her Mindful Gauge to notice her reaction, she has figured out that this is her ideal spot for feeling safe and stable.

Whenever Rodney, Alisha's partner, has a meeting where he feels he may be put under pressure or scrutiny from someone, he makes sure to choose a chair that is not facing a window, which might obscure his vision and trigger a memory of being in an interrogation.

In Vanessa's therapy room there are a number of chairs. Once she has pointed out her seat, she encourages clients to experiment and test out which chair feels best to sit in. One of her clients chooses a different seat each week, illustrating how individual preferences can change. Another chose the same seat for months and then suddenly chose a different seat and reported feeling an instant improvement in mood.

You may have noticed already some of the seemingly smaller things in everyday life that help you to feel calm or more stable. Nevertheless, this exercise can be a good way to become aware or increase awareness you already have.

METHOD

1. Examine the diagram of a room, below. Imagine yourself sitting in each chair. Use your Mindful Gauge to notice your reaction to sitting in each chair.

2. Notice which position you imagine sitting in brings the greatest sense of calm and stability, and notice if you would want to move a chair to a different spot than how they are arranged in this diagram..

3. You may wish to test this out with real chairs in your home, or the next time you are visiting a friend or waiting to see a doctor. Do the spots that feel safest have any similar features, such as facing the door, being by a window, or being set apart from other chairs?

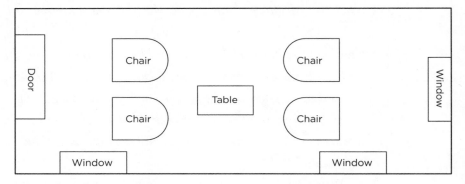

4. If you do notice a pattern, you may choose to test it out in other situations where you are sitting, for example, at cafés and restaurants. As you arrive, take a look around and briefly imagine sitting in the different spots around. Use your Mindful Gauge to work out your preference. Be open to the possiblity of making a mistake. All learning processes involve hits and misses along the way, what is commonly called a learning curve.

5. Getting good at choosing the best chair for you might increase your sense of calm and control in difficult meetings, in interviews, or in therapy sessions. Apply this Goldilocks-like method throughout your daily life to become aware of your preferences that enable you to feel calm and more stable.

Make notes in the space below on what you have discovered about your seating preferences. Check the statements that apply to you.

- ☐ I feel most calm sitting near the door.
- ☐ I feel most calm sitting facing the door.
- ☐ I feel most calm with my back to the door.
- ☐ I feel most calm near a window.
- ☐ I feel most calm facing away from the window.
- ☐ I feel most calm facing a window.
- ☐ I feel most calm with my back to a wall.
- ☐ I feel most calm away from a window.
- ☐ I feel most calm sitting close to someone else.
- ☐ I feel most calm sitting apart from others.

Any other preferences you noticed:

Are these preferences the same in your home? At work? In a restaurant? With different people present?

FIND STABILITY THROUGH BALANCE

When she was younger, Vanessa often balanced objects. She balanced a pen on her finger when she was bored at school and spent hours balancing rocks on top of each other on the beach. In the United Kingdom, a common race at school Sports Day is the egg-and-spoon race, where runners must balance an egg (or, often, a ping-pong-ball substitute) on a spoon and run 100 meters without dropping it. This was Vanessa's favorite race. These balancing activities brought a sense of calm, mastery, and focus that enabled both present-moment awareness and an oasis of distraction from difficult feelings.

Balancing objects employs multiple senses: sight, proprioception (knowing where your body is in space), and vestibular sense (balancing). This means that balancing an object can really hold your attention. However, balancing can also involve some level of frustration if you do too much too soon. In Key 6 we will explore the importance of splitting tasks into small steps. We encourage you to keep it simple, and to use your Mindful Gauge to keep awareness of whether this is bringing more calm focus or whether the level of difficulty needs to be reduced. Or, as with any exercise, whether this is not useful for you.

The purpose here is not to become an expert balancer! The point is to use balance as a way to focus and be present. The level of difficulty will be different for each person. Your balancing abilities may change; adapt the exercise using different objects so that it is challenge enough to hold your attention while also not being too much challenge that it causes distress.

ONE-OBJECT BALANCE

1. Take a pen, or other regular-shaped object, and find the center.
2. Balance it across your index finger.
3. Keep readjusting it until you are able to balance it for longer periods of time.
4. You may naturally start experimenting with moving your hand or your finger to keep the balance.

TWO-OBJECT BALANCE

1. Find two objects. Cuboids are ideal as they offer some easier and more challenging options, and kids' building blocks are great.
2. Balance one on top of the other while holding the base block. To start with, try the long flat edges balanced; once you find that easy, experiment with different sides.
3. As you balance the objects, use your Mindful Gauge to assess the balance between a feeling of calm and the level of challenge and focus the task requires.

We will explore this balance exercise more in Key 7.

CREATIVE, CALMING PATTERNS

Creativity, combined with focus, can offer many people a sense of calm and stability. Mandalas are used in Hindu, Jainist, Shintoist, and Buddhist traditions, yet, like mindfulness, are not limited to religious practices. In fact, there are similar circular, symmetrical designs used in many cultures, including Native American dreamcatchers, Celtic spirals, and Christian rosaries.

Mandalas tend to be circular, but are sometimes square, geometric patterns. Starting from the center of the circle and working your way outward, you create layer after layer of symmetrical patterns.

You may choose to follow the instructions for creating your own mandala. Alternatively, a quick internet search will likely offer you a range of designs to color in. Vanessa enjoys making mandalas with natural materials, gathering leaves and flowers to place in symmetrical rings. She finds it incredibly soothing and stabilizing to take her time to place each one according to its size and color, noticing the intricate detail of the natural materials she has collected.

METHOD

Drawing Mandalas:

In the segments of the circles drawn below, add symbols, colors, or doodles that have a symmetrical pattern around each concentric ring, as shown in the example.

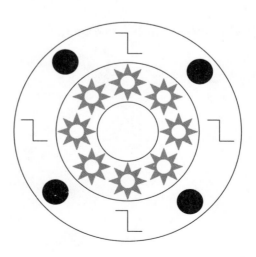

It can be as detailed or as simple as you like. Choose colors and symbols that represent a feeling of calm for you.

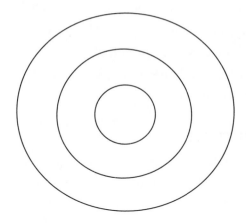

Nature or Object Mandalas:

1. Collect items from your home, from your garden, or on a walk that appeal to you.

   They could be items that symbolize a sense of calm for you or items that you like the shape or color or texture of.

   Around your home, you might choose jewelry or ornaments that bring you a sense of connection, calm, and safety. Outdoors, you could choose pine cones, colorful leaves, interestingly shaped sticks, or flowers.

2. Starting at the center, make a small circle of objects.

3. Keep adding layers outside the center circle. Take your time to choose the objects that you put next to each other. There is no "right way," only what feels and looks right to you.

4. When you have finished, take some time to look at and appreciate your creation. If it is outdoors, you might want to leave it where it is, or you may choose to dismantle it carefully, piece by piece.

NOTICING YOUR STABLE BREATH

How you are breathing can be a reliable indicator of how you are feeling. If you start to feel stressed or worried, it is likely that your breathing will change. Paying attention to these fluctuations may help you take action and gain control, enlisting your stabilizing tools, before you get overwhelmed.

METHOD

1. Take a moment to notice what your breathing is like now.

   What is the rhythm like, and is your belly moving more or less than your chest?

Feeling Stable/Calm	Belly moves more than chest
	Gasping
	Mostly through nostrils
	Inhale longer than exhale
Feeling Stressed	Belly moves more than chest
	Gasping
	Mostly through nostrils
	Inhale longer than exhale
Feeling Afraid	Belly moves more than chest
	Gasping
	Mostly through nostrils
	Inhale longer than exhale
Feeling Exhausted/Fatigued	Belly moves more than chest
	Gasping
	Mostly through nostrils
	Inhale longer than exhale

Is the movement noticeable (deep breathing) or barely perceptible (shallow breathing)?

2. In the table below, circle any of the statements that describe what your breath tends to be like when you feel calm, stressed, afraid, exhausted.

Are there any other descriptions? If so, note them in the blank spaces in the table.

It is likely you will need to pay more attention to your breathing over the course of a day or a week before you can fill this in. Reading through it now will give you an idea of characteristics to look for.

Chest moves more than belly	Smooth	Exhale longer than inhale
Steady	Slow	Fast
Mostly through mouth	Quiet	Loud
Exhale and inhale same length		
Chest moves more than belly	Smooth	Exhale longer than inhale
Steady	Slow	Fast
Mostly through mouth	Quiet	Loud
Exhale and inhale same length		
Chest moves more than belly	Smooth	Exhale longer than inhale
Steady	Slow	Fast
Mostly through mouth	Quiet	Loud
Exhale and inhale same length		
Chest moves more than belly	Smooth	Exhale longer than inhale
Steady	Slow	Fast
Mostly through mouth	Quiet	Loud
Exhale and inhale same length		

USING YOUR BREATH TO STABILIZE

Have you noticed that when you are calm, your exhale tends to be longer than your inhale, and when you are stressed, the inhale tends to be longer? That would be the norm, but as with anything else, it can work the other way around too. What is normal for you?

For many people, purposefully lengthening the exhalation can elicit a feeling of calm. You might have seen runners do just that before they step onto the starting line before a race. Often, they will exhale through pursed lips. This helps lengthen their exhale, helping them calm their nerves and focus on the race.

Note: If your breathing pattern is your most reliable Mindful Gauge, then it might be better to skip this exercise and continue using it as an indicator rather than as a calming strategy. Notice whether that applies to you; if it does, then this exercise might not be right for you at the moment.

METHOD

In the table below are some suggestions of ways to help you lengthen your exhale. If you know or discover that a lengthened exhale helps you feel calmer and more stable, then one or more of these strategies might be helpful. Many are used in yoga classes. If you find this exercise useful and want to explore more, then pranayama, a yogic breath practice, might be worth exploring. Some singing groups also employ breathing techniques, and singing itself is a great way to lengthen your exhale.

Singing

Singing and making vocal sounds tend to lengthen your exhalation without you needing to think about it much. So if you feel a little nervous about focusing on your breath then this might be a good option for you.

Choose a song that gives you a calm or pleasant feeling when you listen to it and sing along!

Vowel Sounds

Making simple vowel sounds can also be useful in lengthening your exhale. For example, "aaah" or "ohhh."

Experiment with taking a few slow breaths, making sound on every or alternate exhales, noticing which feels most calming.

Breathe

Belly Breathing

When in a calm state, the movement of breath tends to happen lower down in your belly; when stressed, breath tends to move your chest more.

Place your hands on your lower belly and take ten breaths, noticing the way your belly moves up and down as you breathe.

Straw Breathing

This is similar to athletes breathing through pursed lips to extend their exhale, and either can work well.

Hold a drinking straw in your hand (do not hold it with your mouth as that may cause tension in your jaw). Breathe normally on your inhale and then exhale through the straw.

Key Review

Did you remember to use your Mindful Gauge to evaluate the exercises in this chapter? If not, was that by choice or because you forgot?

	Did this exercise help, or make you feel worse?	If it helped, what reaction did you have that told you it helped? (For example, felt calmer or stronger or more present.)
Which Phase Is Most Useful for You Right Now?		
Trauma Types		
Pros and Cons		
Safety and Stability Wish List		
Routines and Rituals		
Stabilization Breaks		
Safe-Place Memory		

If you forgot, consider whether you want to go back and do that.
Once you have completed an exercise you may wish to jot down your response and its effectiveness for you in the table.

If it helped, could it be adapted to help more? How?	If it helped, when do you plan to use it?	If it did not help, could you change or adapt it to better suit you? How?

	Did this exercise help, or make you feel worse?	If it helped, what reaction did you have that told you it helped? (For example, felt more calm or stronger or more present.)
What Does Feeling Safe and Stable Mean to You?		
Make a Date With Calm		
Choosing the Right Chair		
Find Stability Through Balance		
Creative, Calming Patterns		
Noticing Your Stable Breath		
Using Your Breath to Stabilize		

If it helped, could it be adapted to help more? How?	If it helped, when do you plan to use it?	If it did not help, could you change or adapt it to better suit you? How?

KEY 4 STOP FLASHBACKS

A *flashback* happens when a memory from the past plays in your mind with such intensity that it *feels* as though the event were happening now. The depiction of traumatic flashbacks is increasingly used to step up story lines of television and movie dramas. You have likely seen several. Of course, these screen depictions can never fully portray the power of a trauma flashback. It is important to realize that a flashback is a memory. However, it is not a simple memory. During a flashback the entire nervous system mimics its previous reaction to the past event, releasing the same hormones and directing the same body responses (increased heart rate, tensed muscles, and so on). It is this nervous system reaction that creates the inner misperception that the traumatic event is happening now or again. Another disturbing feature of flashbacks is that they intrude uninvited, causing confusion and a sense of being out of control.

Normally, people get cues about their surroundings through their five senses: what they hear, taste, see, touch, and smell. At a subconscious level the mind uses that information to evaluate whether a situation is safe or dangerous. For example, your sense of sight helps you to identify whether someone's body posture is threatening or nonthreatening, your sense of smell will alert you to check whether your toast is burning, your sense of hearing will help you to distinguish whether a noise coming from your child's bedroom needs your attention. Routine use of the five senses will help you to quickly evaluate the reality of any situation.

The cues about what is happening inside your body come from internal sensations: whether you are hungry or thirsty, your heart rate has quickened, or your muscles are aching. Internal knowledge includes balance and the ability to recognize where your body (including your hands, arms, feet, and legs) is in space. This knowledge, called proprioception, is why, if you close your eyes, you can probably still touch the tip of your nose with your finger.

Something different happens with many survivors of trauma. Their cues for danger and safety are not taken so much from the external environment, but from their internal sensations. If they feel butterflies in their belly, or their heart quickens or skips a beat, they often conclude there must be something to be afraid of. But there is a problem with that: Internal sensations *cannot* identify danger or safety in your environment, only external senses can do that. Relying on information from internal sensations to judge external safety or danger can lead to big problems. For example, someone might feel absolute terror from a flashback that elicits lots of distressing internal sensations at the same time as they are actually completely safe in their current environment. Likewise, actual danger could be missed due to paying more attention to the internal cues than the external ones. When otherwise neutral stimuli cause this kind of confusion, they are called *triggers*. These are usually unexpected external stimuli, such as a sound, a color, a type of clothing, a particular odor, and so on, that have become associated with the traumatic memory. That kind of link can cause the nervous system to automatically react as though the threat of the past were happening again. It is impossible to completely avoid such triggers, because they are usually things that you come across in your everyday life that inadvertently have a sensory connection to the traumatic memory (such as a color, odor, or shape). However, you can gain control of your reaction to triggers through learning to notice where and when you frequently encounter them and then applying strategies presented in this chapter. That way you will be able to control them instead of them controlling you.

What Can Help

Some people worry that flashbacks are something that simply must be endured. However, they are not necessary or even helpful. Flashbacks do not help you recover from trauma. Actually, they can make healing more difficult. Controlling flashbacks will help you recognize that your traumatic experience is now in your past, not your present. That will also help you to connect with your feelings in a healthy way, rather than being overwhelmed by them.

In the pages that follow there is a range of exercises that are intended to help you to develop greater awareness of and differentiation between internal and external information so you can better evaluate your situation at any given moment in time. Even if you do not suffer from flashbacks, many of the exercises in this chapter may, nonetheless, be useful for you. Read through all of them first and then decide which are relevant for you.

This is a reminder for you to use your Mindful Gauge with the exercises below. You might find the Mindful Gauge to be a handy tool for you. Alternatively, the idea of it might inspire you to an evaluation method of your own design.

First, check with your Mindful Gauge how it feels to read the exercise. If it feels okay, continue the exercise, and continue to check in. Then check your Mindful Gauge afterwards. Do you feel better or worse? Is this a good resource for you?

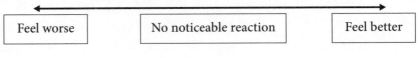

| Feel worse | No noticeable reaction | Feel better |

INTERNAL AND EXTERNAL

One step toward gaining mastery over flashbacks involves applying mindfulness to recognize where and how you are at any given moment in your present life. That will help you to know that the trauma happened in the past and that the flashback is a memory of it. The quickest link to that present moment is through the use of one or more of your five senses: sight, hearing, touch, smell, and taste. They will help you to know and be aware of your actual surroundings from one moment to the next.

Being aware of your surroundings using your five senses can help you to assess for safety when your body might be reacting to a trigger. Notice your body reaction—maybe tight muscles, or faster breathing—and then notice what is going on that might have elicited that response. Is it something actually in your environment, or was it internal, like a thought or a body sensation such as hunger? Actually look, listen, and smell your current environment for cues to right now. For example, as you are reading this book, take a moment to look around where you are and identify several things (lights, chairs, doors, and so on), listen to noises inside and outside the place where you are, notice any odors or aromas.

Of course, if you are in danger in the present, **seek safety**. However, if you are safe keep reading or carrying on with whatever you were doing. The same process applies if you become triggered, with the addition of making a note of the trigger and your reaction to it.

METHOD

Internal: Color, draw symbols, or write words to represent how you feel inside your body right now.

External: Looking all around you in your environment, including above you and below you, list as many things as possible that you can see/hear/smell/feel/taste right now.

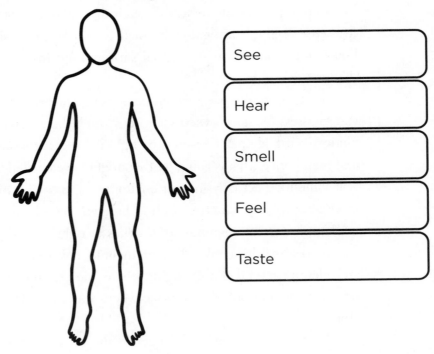

See

Hear

Smell

Feel

Taste

EXTRA GUIDANCE: Track what you notice. Do you get the same body reaction when you smell, see, hear, feel, or taste the same or a similar thing?

SELF-TALK: THAT WAS A MEMORY

Many people experiencing flashbacks speak as though the flashback were occurring in the present. They often use present-tense verbs to describe their flashback experience. The use of present-tense language is unhelpful, as it reinforces the erroneous belief that a memory could be the same as an actual event happening again or still. Whether out loud or internally, your internal dialogue might be along the lines of "I'm here again," "I see the car," or "I can smell the smoke." Control of your flashbacks will further be gained through editing your internal dialogue, including using past-tense verbs to describe a flashback—to tell the truth, that it is a memory of the past: "I was there," "I saw the car," or "I smelled the smoke."

Notice your self-talk when you have intrusive memories. Do you talk about them as though they are in the past or as if they are happening now? Notice how you could change your self-talk to past tense to reinforce to your system that what happened then is not happening now, that you have survived and what you are feeling is a response to a memory.

It may help to write down your inner dialogue in this way, turning the present-tense sentences into past tense. The physical aspect of writing, as well as seeing the words written down, may help to reinforce to your nervous system that you are reacting to a memory.

> **CAUTION:** This is *not* an exercise to record or write all about your memory itself. The goal here is to help you reinforce that what happened is past, part of your history.

Alter statements about the past from present-tense language to past-tense language. Read your alteration over.

Example: I hear the explosion.	I heard the explosion.
Example: I hear the explosion now.	It reminds me of when I heard the explosion.
Example: I can hear the explosion.	The loud noise of the car reminds me of the explosion I *heard* twenty years ago.

MANTRA: THAT WAS A MEMORY

A flashback is a memory. Regardless of how intense and powerful that flashback seems, it is still a memory. Even though it can be overwhelming, terrifying, and can cause an extreme reaction through your whole system, it is, nonetheless, a memory.

Most people experience flashbacks as a loss of control, as the flashback being in charge. The good news is that it is definitely possible to take control of flashbacks. To do so, the vital first step is to recognize a basic truth: A flashback is a memory, no matter how intense or real it seems.

You may wish to find a mantra that you can write down and keep in your pocket, such as:

> That was a memory. As real as it may have felt, it is not happening now.

Try out some different ways of writing this that feel right to you. It may feel good to simply write "That was a memory" several times.

Keep the sentences short and do not include any details of your trauma (otherwise you could risk intensifying a flashback rather than dampening it).

EMPOWER OBJECTS

Following a nightmare, or during a panic attack or flashback, you may feel disoriented about whether you are in the present or not. One strategy, used by many, is to empower one or more objects as "now objects" so that when you see or touch them, you will be confident that you are in the present, not the past.

Empower objects as "now objects" so that when you see them, you know that you are in the present day. Keep at least one in your pocket, by your bedside, anywhere such a reminder might come in handy.

- Something with a recent date on it, such as a coin or a newspaper. You can read the date out loud to reinforce that you are here, now.
- A souvenir of a pleasant place, for example, a flat penny from an enjoyable holiday, a pebble from a favorite beach.
- Anything that you own now that you did not at the time of the traumatic event. That might be a phone, a book, a bracelet, or a badge.
- A small gift or token from someone who cares about you.

OTHER ANCHORS TO NOW

As well as empowering your "now objects," it might be useful to do any of the following:

- Check the date on a calendar or phone.
- Read through the Be Here, Now exercises in Key 1 and your Timeline from Key 2.
- Clap your hands, stamp your feet, speak, or sing out loud.
- Look outside the window.
- Listen to the traffic on the street or the dog barking next door.
- Go to the kitchen and taste or smell something.

Feel free to be creative in identifying or making your own.

PRESENT-DAY FACT SHEET

The more reminders you have of your present, the more proof you will have to ground you in the here and now.

METHOD

1. Make a list of facts about you and your life that are only applicable to you *now*.
2. Keep copies of this list on your phone, in your pockets, by your bed, and so on, to read through.

Focus on what is different now from in the past.

- the current date
- where you live
- your age
- who you live with
- pets you have
- shoe size
- phone type
- computer model
- hobbies
- people you know
- qualifications you have
- type or color of car/ transport
- clothing size
- length of hair
- favorite song
- your son/pet/favorite movie star/ friend is ____ years old
- your job

Examples for your Anchors to Now list are on the next page.

My Present-Day Fact Sheet

The year is _____

I am _____ years old

I live in _____

My car is a _____

I live with _____

My shoe size is _____

_____

_____

_____

_____

_____

_____

_____

_____

_____

_____

_____

_____

_____

_____

BEING HERE, NOW KIT

Bringing your awareness to the present moment is a powerful way to take control of flashbacks. Although during a flashback you can feel as though you have been transported to the past or that it is happening again, that is not true. A flashback is not a time machine, no matter how real that feeling may be. The key to identifying and being sure that the flashback is a memory about the past is to use your senses to identify your external surroundings so you are able to distinguish between now and then. That will also help you to assess whether you are actually in danger or are safe.

Having a kit of things that bring your awareness back to the present can be useful. Start with too many. That way, as you are testing out what works best you can gradually weed out what does not work as well. Alternatively, you may find more things to add. Regularly review and adapt your kit to suit what is most useful for you. Below are some ideas to start you off; make sure to add your own:

- something soft to touch
- a small vial or bottle with something good to smell
- a few candies to taste
- a file card or two with a few written cues to the present: "A flashback is a memory," "I survived," and such

Make a list of things to gather to put in your own bag. You might find inspiration using the tools you found effective in the Being Here, Now exercises in Key 1.

Pleasant and grounding things to touch/feel (e.g., a soft blanket, an interesting object, a precious stone).

Pleasant and ground things to hear (e.g., make your own grounding playlist on your phone, a little bell that jingles as you move).

Pleasant and grounding things to taste (e.g., something sweet or sour).

Pleasant and grounding things to smell (e.g., drops of an essential oil on a handkerchief).

Pleasant and grounding things to look at (e.g., a photograph of a dear friend, something that symbolizes strength and grounding for you).

Written protocols, written anchors to now, calming poems (e.g., Flashback Protocol in this Key).

PROTECTIVE BOUNDARIES

Visualizing a protective boundary around you may give or add to your feeling of strength. Note: This exercise relies on imagination. Everyone is different in how they imagine. Some picture what things look like, others are more likely to imagine sounds or what something feels like. Play to your strength (always!). Even though the instruction may involve visual imagery, feel free to translate that into auditory imagery or the feeling you have in your body or on your skin. And, of course, if this (or any) exercise does not appeal to you, skip it altogether or return to it later.

METHOD

1. Notice whether there is a particular color, texture, or even sound that comes to mind when you think or read the word "protection," and imagine that color, texture, or sound around your body.

2. Pay attention to how wide and dense what you are imagining needs to be for you to feel protected. Would you like to add layers of different colors, textures, or sounds?

3. Are there images that you associate with protection? For example, a bubble all around you that can repel anything unwanted, flowering green vines circling you, a moat, a razor-wire fence, a castle wall, a mountain range, a babbling brook, and so on. Add one of these to your protective boundary. Is there one of these that feels more protective than another? Do both of them together feel stronger than each alone? Do you want to keep one or the other in your resource kit?

4. Which sensory features bring you a sense of safety and protection? Imagine what your boundary smells, feels, sounds, or tastes like.

5. How close or far away would you like your boundary to be from your body? You can play with the sense of your boundary when you are alone and when you are with others. For instance, maybe having the boundary tighter to your body and firmer would be nice in a more enclosed space, like an elevator or a busy train. Experiment with moving your boundary with your command: in, out, up, down, thinner, thicker, and so on.

6. Are there differences when you feel wrapped in this protection and when you do not? How do your body and feelings respond?

Using the suggestions above, describe your imagined protective boundary here:

If imagining this protective boundary feels helpful to you, you might practice it each day. As with anything else, the more you practice, the quicker and more easily the image and feeling of it will come when you feel you need it most. It may be useful to be able to imagine your boundary with your eyes open so that you can have your visual sense to support staying present and so that you can use it when you also need your eyes, for example, to walk or drive safely.

DRAW YOUR PROTECTIVE BOUNDARY

Art speaks where words are unable to explain.

— MATHIOLE

METHOD

1. Use colors, symbols, and images that feel protective to create a boundary around the body image below.
2. You can draw or cut-and-paste images or colors from a newspaper or magazine.
3. Feel free to add words if you like, such as "I choose who I let in," "I'll decide in my own time." Choose *only* those statements that bring you a *greater sense of calm* or *strength*.

When you have finished with your boundary picture, notice how you feel looking at it. Which aspects of your Mindful Gauge (Key 1) are activated? If your gauge suggests this is useful, looking at your drawing at the start of, or throughout, the day might be something you add to your routine.

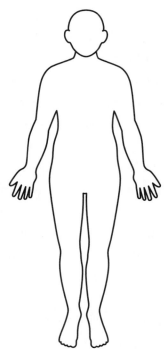

FLASHBACK TRIGGERS
AND RESOURCES

When you are triggered to the memory of a traumatic event, your internal system reacts as if you were in danger again so that you can protect yourself. However, sometimes this fantastic protection system gets it wrong. For example, if a person involved in your trauma was wearing something orange at the time, seeing something orange in the present might trigger the memory, but, of course, that does not mean you are in danger now, even though your body might react as if you were.

Rubi noticed that although she loved to ride her bicycle, particularly up in the hills, she often became overwhelmed and frequently had flashbacks of an earlier traumatic situation. She was reluctant to acknowledge that her beloved cycling was causing the flashbacks because cycling usually made her feel powerful and strong. She did not want to give it up, but she also wanted to stop the flashbacks.

Through mindful attention and keeping a log of her reactions, she realized that the sound of her quickened breath pedaling up the hills reminded her of the breathless fright she had felt those many years ago. Once she identified that being out of breath was a trigger to her flashback, she began to take control.

Rubi found that she had several choices. She could cycle slower so she did not get out of breath, listen to music in earphones so she could not hear her breath, or prepare for the trigger by using calming skills before and during the ride. She also used her five senses to pay attention to how different her surroundings were while cycling compared to the time of the traumatic event, and created a mantra to remind her that being out of breath from pleasant cycling was quite different from breathless fright. As a result, her feelings of self-control, strength, and power grew tremendously, not only through the cycling but also by her mastery over the cycling-induced flashback trigger.

In this exercise you will identify your common triggers so that you can become familiar with them or, if necessary, avoid them. Bringing awareness to triggers will help you to separate past from present: "Ah, because of the past, I know that pink crayons make my system think I'm in danger—thanks for protecting me, I'll use all my five senses to check whether I am in danger right now or am reacting to that memory of danger." Knowing your triggers will provide you with clues as to why you are reacting and help you to take charge and stabilize your system.

METHOD

In the table below, make a note of the stimuli that trigger flashbacks and the resources you use that help you take control. You may notice a pattern, such as a time of day, a particular place, a sound, a color—it could be just about anything. For example, if you notice that traveling on the subway or bus is a trigger, you could try walking, cycling, or driving instead for a while. Sometimes you might not know what triggered a flashback. Be patient; detective work can take a little time. Jot down a note or two about it. As a little time passes, the stimulus may occur to you.

FLASHBACK TRIGGERS
AND RESOURCES

Trigger	Day, time, and location	Sensory type of trigger (see/hear/smell/taste/feel)	What was the reaction to the trigger?	
			Thoughts/mind images	Body sensations

Emotions/mood	What resources helped you back to your comfort zone?	Where/when would contact with this trigger be most likely?	What resources might help next time?

NOTICING PATTERNS

Rubi gained control of her flashbacks by identifying her triggers, tracking when she was most likely to come across them, and experimenting with what helped. Use the completed table in the previous exercise to evaluate what you have learned.

Refer to the table in the previous exercise.

Do you notice any patterns? Are there regular days, times, or places where the flashbacks most occur?

Which resources did you notice bring you to the present or out of a flashback the quickest?

MAKING A PLAN

Having a solid plan to preempt your flashbacks may enable you to gain control. Not only will you be able to avoid the circumstances where possible, you will also be more likely to be able to use your tools and resources to stay present and in charge.

METHOD

Use your Mindful Gauge from Key 1 to determine which resources from your toolbox will be most effective before, during, and following the different situations where you foresee potential to have a flashback.

Using the information from your table, when are you likely to have a flashback?	Which resources will you use to help you feel strong, calm, and present *before entering* that situation?	Which resources may *keep you present* when in that situation?	What resources will you use to bring you *back into the present* if you have a flashback in that situation?

TAKING CONTROL OF YOUR FLASHBACK

The biggest problem with flashbacks is that they feel like they are in charge, that they control you. This exercise set will teach you how to take charge of your flashbacks to put yourself in control. You can approach this procedure several ways, choosing the steps and structures that best suit you. Through practice, evaluation, adjustment, more practice, and reevaluation, you will design your own procedure that will help you to

- stop a flashback;
- reduce the impact of a flashback;
- prepare for a situation you are facing that you anticipate could trigger a flashback;
- create a morning ritual that will increase your ability to quickly and automatically take control of a flashback (the way a fire drill in school prepares schoolchildren to react safely in the event of a real fire); and
- teach a friend or family member how to coach you to stop a flashback.

Once you have developed your own set of steps, you can decide if you want to

- keep copies or reminders of it visible in key places;
- practice it at regular intervals, when you are not having a flashback, so that it becomes second nature;
- record your sequence on your mobile phone or other recording device to be available at the push of a button; and
- create additional strategies to remind yourself that you can take control at any time.

METHOD

Suggested steps are outlined below. They are not numbered because it is up to you to choose and order them as best helps you. Also feel free to add one or more steps that you come up with yourself. Just make sure to stick with the main goal: to control and stop your flashback.

Use your own knowledge and your Mindful Gauge to help you choose and edit your procedure into something that absolutely suits you. Try it different ways and see what works best for you. If, for example, you become more distressed when sensing your body, skip that step or insert another. Set aside, but do not throw out, any of the steps you do not use, as you may find them useful at a later stage in your recovery. The same for any you create yourself but determine are not for you right now.

However, there are two steps that are essential. You can say them in your own words and insert them in the order that makes the most sense to you; just make sure to stay true to the essence of each:

ESSENTIAL STEP 1

"What I am experiencing now is a *memory*. No matter how real it feels, it is a memory and is not happening now."

"I am (afraid, shaky, spaced out—whatever) right now because I am *remembering* _____."

Make sure you fill in the blank very briefly, not more than 2 or 3 words.

That is because you are working to stop the flashback, *not* go into it.

ESSENTIAL STEP 2

Shift attention to your external senses and name at least 3 things you can see, hear, and/or smell *right now*:

"I hear the lawn mower next door."
"I see the sun shining through the front window."
"I smell cinnamon from the bread in the toaster."

Continue to notice and name external senses until you feel your awareness is securely tied to your actual present environment.

In addition to the steps above, you can add any or all of the following:

> Identify what you are feeling emotionally, for example, "I am afraid."

> Affirm today's date, including the year, month, and day.

> Pay attention to your internal senses, naming one or more sensations you have, such as heart rate, changes in respiration, dizziness, sweaty palms, shaky legs, cold hands, or butterflies in your stomach.

Lastly, based on the information from the above steps, evaluate whether the situation you are in *now* is safe or dangerous.

If you are indeed safe, despite having a flashback, you can then tell yourself,

> *"I am having a flashback and I am not in any danger."*
> *Or "[the title of the trauma] is not happening now (or again)."*

If you are not in safe circumstances, make sure to **seek safety**.

Here is an example of an individualized flashback-stopping procedure. Remember, yours will be different. Just be sure to include the pertinent elements.

> "What I am experiencing now is a *memory*. No matter how real it feels, it is a memory and not happening now.
>
> I am really scared, my heart is racing, and I am shivering cold, **because I am remembering** the attack when I was 10.
>
> At the same time, **I am looking** around my living room **in 2021** and **I can see** my green couch, my flat-screen television, and my husband's shoes.
>
> **I can also hear** the microwave beeping that the leftovers are warm and **I can hear** my son yelling at his sister.
>
> **By the calendar I can see** it is 30 years later. **So, I know** that the attack was a long time ago, that I survived, and **that it is *not* happening now (or again)**."

Below, write your own sequence of steps to control and stop your flashback. Read it through a few times using your Mindful Gauge to check whether it feels right. Copy it out and put it in multiple places where you can easily find it.

Key Review

Did you remember to use your Mindful Gauge to evaluate the exercises in this chapter? If not, was that by choice or because you forgot?

	Did this exercise help, or make you feel worse?	If it helped, what reaction did you have that told you it helped? (For example, felt calmer or stronger or more present.)
Internal and External		
Self-Talk: That Was a Memory		
Mantra: That Was a Memory		
Empower Objects		
Other Anchors to Now		
Present-Day Fact Sheet		

If you forgot, consider whether you want to go back and do that.

Once you have completed an exercise you may wish to jot down your response and its effectiveness for you in the table.

If it helped, could it be adapted to help more? How?	If it helped, when do you plan to use it?	If it did not help, could you change or adapt it to better suit you? How?

	Did this exercise help, or make you feel worse?	If it helped, what reaction did you have that told you it helped? (For example, felt calmer or stronger or more present.)
Being Here, Now Kit		
Protective Boundaries		
Draw Your Protective Boundary		
Flashback Triggers and Resources		
Noticing Patterns		
Making a Plan		
Taking Control of Your Flashback		

If it helped, could it be adapted to help more? How?	If it helped, when do you plan to use it?	If it did not help, could you change or adapt it to better suit you? How?

KEY 5A RECONCILE FORGIVENESS AND SHAME

Forgive Your Limitations

Forgiveness of others is often regarded as an important aspect of trauma recovery. However, that is a misnomer. It is absolutely *not* essential to forgive others in order for you to recover.

Where there are one or more key people at fault, *choosing* to forgive one or more of them might be beneficial for you, but that needs to be your choice. Unfortunately, many trauma survivors report feeling pushed to forgive or an internal obligation to do so, with an insinuation that if they do not forgive then they are a bad or weak person or that they will not recover. This type of forced or coerced forgiveness of others is unlikely to offer any therapeutic benefit, and can actually create increased feelings of shame and self-blame. Forgiveness must be an individual choice for it to be of any benefit. It is another area where you can take control, deciding for yourself whether forgiveness is a good idea for you.

As you can find many books that recommend forgiveness of others, the focus of this chapter is on the much neglected, though often essential, aspect of trauma recovery: *self*-forgiveness.

Carla and her children were rescued from an apartment-building fire in the middle of the night by firefighters. The source of the blaze was the kitchen in a neighbor's apartment on a lower floor. With no safe escape route, they had to wait for the firefighters to arrive, which was immeasur-

ably distressing. Carla shouted for help, tried to keep her children calm and hopeful, and waited for the rescue team to arrive. Following the fire, Carla felt that she had not done enough to protect herself or her children, and she developed intense feelings of guilt about this. Though she had indisputable evidence that the fire was not her fault, the fact that she and her children were trapped on an upper floor, too high to jump from, made it difficult for her to accept that she could not have done more.

As with Carla, it can sometimes be difficult to accept that during your trauma you were not in control and were unable to prevent what happened to you. This can lead to a feeling that it was your fault. In this Key we shall explore some of the physiological, neurological, and emotional responses to trauma in the hope that it may deepen your understanding of why you were unable to respond as you might have expected or wanted. We hope that having a better understanding of these involuntary and usually unconscious mechanisms will help you toward self-forgiveness. As written in the introduction, there are few hard facts in life; however, this is one: Trauma does not happen if someone is in control. If they are not in the wrong place at the wrong time, or unable to stop the car, or to prevent the assault, they will not suffer lasting trauma. Therefore, everyone with traumatic stress that continues to intrude on their daily life already knows what it is like to be out of control. And then, in the aftermath of trauma, there can be physical, emotional, and psychological symptoms that feel beyond a person's control—like, for example, the triggers or flashbacks that seem as if they control you. So, it makes perfect sense that survivors of trauma often need to feel in control in various ways. Fearing losing control again, and tolerating the uncertainty of what might happen in the future, can, for many, be difficult to bear. For some, feeling guilty can be a coping strategy that protects them from those feelings. Holding yourself responsible for what happened may give you a feeling of power or control about a situation where in fact you were powerless.

Carla believed that holding herself accountable, and identifying things that she could have done differently or better, helped her to feel safer when worrying about potential similar scenarios in the future.

Though it was not pleasant to feel guilty, it seemed reassuring that if the same happened again, maybe she could act differently so that she and her children would suffer less.

(Caveat: If it is actually true that someone is responsible for their trauma—for example, they robbed a bank and were traumatized by their arrest and incarceration—then it is important for them to take responsibility and work toward repairing the wrong they did. However, this chapter is not written for those in such circumstances.)

Everyone has limitations. No one can manage every situation and prevent all adversity. Accepting your own limitations, rather than holding yourself to blame, is difficult for many people. An important question is: Did you actually have a choice? In most cases trauma happens because people do not have a choice. That is why they are often called *victims*.

Facing her limitations meant that Carla had to come to terms with the fact that there are some things in her life that are beyond her control. Though accepting this was difficult, doing so freed her from the shame and guilt that were impacting her quality of life in the present. Identifying what she could not control also helped her to distinguish where she really did have control and where she could strengthen her sense of control, including exploring the resources she already had, and aiming to add those that she wanted to gain.

Generally, it is the amygdala, in the middle part of your brain, that directs how your body responds to trauma: whether you flee, fight, or freeze. Following trauma, it is the limbic system that continues to activate those body responses when you get triggered or have a flashback. That is the basis of most trauma symptoms. However, for those of you who wish your body had reacted differently or would like your body to react differently now, it may help to know that to some degree it can be possible to reprogram or update your amygdala by teaching your body additional ways to react when threatened. Though it is not a guarantee, by expanding your resources there is a greater potential for the amygdala to employ a different strategy, for example, running or fighting instead of freezing.

Many people who have been assaulted, for example, reprogram

their amygdala by taking self-defense training, or by increasing aerobic exercise or strength training. However, the amygdala always chooses the strategy most likely to help you survive in that moment, even if it is not the strategy that the cognitive, thinking part of your brain would have preferred. That is one of the reasons that in Key 3 we celebrated the fact that the amygdala did its job: You survived!

Remember Your Mindful Gauge

As with all the exercises in this book, we encourage you to read through the following exercises first and use your Mindful Gauge (from Key 1) to help you decide which ones seem good for you to try. Continue to use your Mindful Gauge as you do each exercise to stay aware of your reaction and decide whether you repeat an exercise, move on to the next one, or do something else.

This is a reminder for you to use your Mindful Gauge with the following exercises. You might find the Mindful Gauge to be a handy tool for you. Alternatively, the idea of it might inspire you to an evaluation method of your own design.

First, check with your Mindful Gauge how it feels to read the exercise. If it feels okay, then continue the exercise, and continue to check in. Make sure to check your Mindful Gauge afterwards. Do you feel better or worse for having tried the exercise? Is it a good resource for you?

| Feel worse | No noticeable reaction | Feel better |

AUTONOMIC NERVOUS SYSTEM RESPONSES

People who froze in response to trauma, including with reactions such as dissociating, going numb, temporary paralysis, or "playing dead," have historically experienced criticism, skepticism, and outright disbelief in courtrooms, in police interviews, and with family members and friends. It is only since around the turn of the 21st century that scientific theory, including as mentioned about the amygdala above, has confirmed that humans respond much as animals in the wild do when their lives are threatened, often involuntarily freezing. If you have also been disbelieving yourself, learning the science might help you toward understanding and self-forgiveness.

SURVIVAL

Humans have developed their available responses to danger as they have evolved, and through the advancement and changes of the brain. It is believed that the first defense against threat was the freeze response, which developed around 500 million years ago. The fight-or-flight response evolved later, around 400 million years ago. The goal of these responses is simple: to survive.

During a traumatic incident, when life is threatened, the amygdala works fast, much faster than your conscious, thinking brain. It likely has already taken in sensory information, analyzed the information, compared it to past experience, and sent information telling your body how to react, before the thinking part of your brain is even fully aware of the danger. This has advantages. Usually, in such situations, the cognitive process of evaluating a situation and making a rational decision about what to do is much too slow to ensure survival; an instant response is necessary, and the amygdala is able to provide this.

You may have seen animals respond to danger, either in person or on film. Vanessa's dog, Gemma, was previously a feral dog and is a swift hunter. On their hikes, Vanessa often watches Gemma's potential prey react instantly: Field mice that were munching on some greenery suddenly take flight as the dog approaches. On one recent frosty morning,

Gemma approached a mouse quickly without it noticing until it was too late, the dog was already too close for the mouse to run. Vanessa witnessed as the mouse collapsed stiffly on the ground. Gemma sniffed it and then, losing interest, padded on without attacking. Once Gemma had passed by, the mouse swiftly came back to life and sped away in the opposite direction. It is common for prey animals to freeze. If they are lucky, as was this mouse, and the predator loses interest, the prey takes advantage to escape. Humans do the same, freezing when a danger is inescapable, usually without voluntary decision-making. For Gemma and other predatory animals, instinctively, the risk of bacterial infection from a seemingly already dead prey is not worth the risk of eating, unless the predator is very hungry. The freeze response, which may initially seem counterintuitive to the cognitive part of the brain, actually saves lives.

Considering Gemma and the mouse, imagine if, instead of the fast automatic amygdala response, the mouse had paused to cognitively consider its options. Gemma would have pounced before the mouse could decide what to do, and it would not have survived.

Here is a human example you might be able to relate to.

Katy suddenly jumped out of her chair. She had been sitting under a balcony when someone accidently dropped their purse over the rail above. It landed right on the table where Katy had been sitting. Her reaction was instantaneous and automatic. She did not think about this reaction, or even consciously notice the sound of the person shouting, "Look out below," until she was already standing a safe distance from the table. Her response was completely unconscious, and driven by the amygdala.

TRAUMA-RESPONSE LIMITATIONS

Some people feel guilty about how their body unconsciously responded in a traumatic event. This might include running away and leaving a friend in a dangerous situation due to a flight response, injuring an attacker if the automatic reaction was a fight response, or even having an involuntary orgasm when molested. Learning the difference between consciously choosing a response and having an unconscious, automatic response to a threat may help you find compassion for how you responded when traumatized.

1. In the tables in the diagram below, write short statements describing your responses to past experiences (use everyday experiences, not traumatic ones).

    Write them in either the Fast Response section or the Slow Response section, depending on how you think you reacted.

    The Fast Response is when you made an instinctual, involuntary reaction, such as Katy jumping out of her chair (your body and brain reacted without your thinking about it).

Fast Response (Amygdala only)				
Sensory Information	A friend approached me from behind in a busy cafe and tapped me on the shoulder	Out of the corner of my eye I saw a glass falling from the kitchen counter		
Response	I jumped out of my chair and screeched	I reached out and caught it		

142 KEYS TO SAFE TRAUMA RECOVERY WORKBOOK

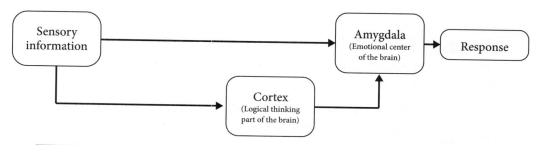

Slow Response (Cortex and Amygdala)				
Sensory Information	I saw my friend enter the cafe and walk over to me	I noticed a glass close to the edge of the kitchen counter		
Response	I thought that they will need space to sit down and moved my bag to create space	I thought that it could easily be knocked off, and moved it to a safer position		

The Slow Response is when you consciously took the information, thought about it, and made a decision based on your considerations. Some examples are given; try to add some of your own in the empty boxes.

2. Consider your immediate responses to your traumatic experience: fight, flight, or freeze. Where would that response sit in these diagrams? It is usual to find that they are in the Fast Response.

3. Using your knowledge of how your brain responds to threat, write a letter of forgiveness to yourself for the immediate response you had to your traumatic experience. You may also wish to include gratitude to your brain for trying to protect you. If this is too difficult to include at the moment, that is absolutely okay; you can always return to this at a later time, or not. Respect what feels right for you.

Reviewing the brain information in Key 2 and Key 4 may help. You may also wish to do some further reading if you notice that it helps you.

Example: I forgive my brain for using the fast route to respond, whereby the thinking part of my brain was shut off. I had flipped my lid due to being terrified. As my cortex was offline, I was not in conscious control of the decision to freeze. I forgive myself for being out of control because of this automatic response. I realize that this is the survival mechanism that everyone has. I did not choose this response. Though I was not able to stop the trauma, I thank my amygdala for trying to protect and save me.

ADDITIONAL LIMITATIONS

In addition to your automatic survival response, there may be numerous circumstantial reasons that limited you in preventing your trauma.

The list below offers some possibilities. Mark the ones that applied to your situation. In reading over the possibilities below, you might think of other ways in which you were limited, or you might wish to phrase something differently. Definitely add any such additions to your list.

I was a child/young.	I was not strong enough.
I was outnumbered.	I made a mistake that I did not purposefully intend.
I was manipulated.	It was an unpreventable act of nature.
I was threatened.	I did not have the help I needed.
My amygdala response to protect me was to freeze/dissociate.	My amygdala response to protect me was to get away.
My amygdala response to protect me was to fight.	Someone made a mistake.
I was not physically big enough.	I was not as fast.
I could not predict the future.	I was afraid.
My body responded involuntarily; I did not choose the response.	My movement was restricted.
I had no knowledge that I was in the wrong place at the wrong time.	

SHOULD HAVE,
WOULD HAVE, COULD HAVE

As you have read this Key, have you become aware of, or been reminded of, any thoughts you have (or have had) about the trauma that caused you to blame yourself for it happening or for the way you responded? These normal expressions of regret often show up as "I should have . . ." or "I wish I would have . . ." or "I could have . . ." Or "I wish I had . . ."

Though you might be trying to protect yourself by thinking of ways you could prevent future trauma, this kind of self-talk can reinforce the idea that you were somehow to blame.

Siobhan was assaulted when she was 10 years old. On her walk home from school, a boy from the local high school attacked her and demanded money. Siobhan froze for long enough that he was able to take the wallet out of her bag, unzip it, take out the money, and push her to the ground before walking away. In the aftermath, she was angry with herself and felt ashamed for not fighting or running away. For many years following the assault and robbery, she gave herself a hard time about what she should have said or done. In her mind, the majority of the blame for the event fell on her rather than the attacker.

Though these self-blaming thoughts ran often through her mind, she did not question them or think about the thoughts themselves. However, in a therapy session when Siobhan was a young adult, the therapist asked her to write down her blaming thoughts and then read what she wrote. When she saw the words in writing, and then spoke them aloud, she realized how much she had blamed herself for that incident. Once she learned that her amygdala, not her cortex, had decided how to react, and then recognized her limited resources at the time (she was much smaller, weaker, and slower than the high school boy), she was finally able to find compassion for her younger self.

METHOD

1. In the Self-Talk column write any beliefs you hold about the trauma. You may wish to use the sentence starters below, or you may already be aware of your own.

   I should . . . / I could . . . / If only I had . . .

2. In the Compassionate Response column use the information from the previous exercises to respond to that self-talk with the facts about your limitations at the time of the incident.

3. In the Self-Forgiving Statement column, write a short statement based on what you know about why you responded the way you did.

To connect with that compassionate response, you may wish to imagine one of your rainbow resources (remember Maya Angelou in Key 2?) saying the sentences in "Self-Talk" to you, and what your response to them might be. Alternatively, it may be helpful to look at a photograph of yourself around the age when the trauma happened. Use your Mindful Gauge to check whether this makes you feel more overwhelmed. Do not use a photograph that includes any reminder of or links to the trauma. The idea is that you get a sense of yourself and your limitations at that time so that you can find compassion for your frozen self. This will not be useful for everyone.

Self-Talk (Usually this includes the words "always," "never," "should," or similar)	Compassionate Response	Self-Forgiving Statement
I should have fought back.	I was a child; I was smaller than him, I was not as strong as him, and my amygdala directed my body outside my cognitive awareness to freeze, as that was my best chance for survival in that situation.	I forgive myself for freezing when he attacked me.
I should have shouted for help.	I was in freeze state and physiologically unable to shout. This was not a choice. My amygdala used the strategy most likely to help me survive.	I forgive myself for my autonomic response.
It is all my fault; if only I had walked a different route.	I did not choose to be attacked and could not have foreseen that.	I forgive myself for not foreseeing the future.

Self-Talk (Usually this includes the words "always," "never," "should," or similar)	Compassionate Response	Self-Forgiving Statement

SHALL, WILL, CAN RESOURCES

It might be useful for you to change the self-talk from the previous exercise into ideas of resources that you would like to develop in the present.

Part of Siobhan's self-blame was because she was trying to find solutions, things that she could do to avoid a similar trauma happening again. She was afraid that exploring her limitations would cement her vulnerabilities and increase her anxiety. However, through examining her beliefs about self-blame and forgiveness Siobhan realized that many of the limitations she had during the trauma were due to things beyond her control, such as the automatic amygdala response and her being a child, which she no longer is.

Siobhan explored how some of the self-talk might also indicate ways in which she still felt vulnerable. That realization gave her the chance to change both how she was talking to herself and how she was reacting to the critical self-talk. Rather than hearing the self-talk as criticism, she began to understand that it was trying to protect her from the trauma happening again. Instead of totally blocking it out, she used it as a guide to find resources that would help her to feel safer. For example, "I should have fought back": She forgave the younger self who did not fight back, due to various limitations, but also realized that she did not currently feel strong enough to defend herself. She decided to take a self-defense class. When she completed the class, she found that feeling stronger and more able in her body was something that she was interested in developing even further. She bought some weights to enhance strength training. The increased tools from the self-defense class, combined with her stronger muscles from strength training, helped her to feel safer. Though the self-talk was unhelpful when she was looking at the past, it gave her ideas of resources that she could develop in the present to better protect herself in the future.

If you find that your own self-talk does not point you toward resources that would be helpful to develop now, it might be most appropriate instead to simply forgive your limitations and look for resource ideas elsewhere.

METHOD

1. Copy the self-talk from the previous exercise.

2. Notice whether the self-talk offers a suggestion about a missing resource that you would like to have or that you feel would benefit you. Add this to the Resources column. Remember that a compassionate response itself might be the resource you have been missing.

3. You may notice that the limitation does not exist anymore at all. For example, if the limitation was that you were a small child and now you are a grown adult, that can be added to the resources that you have now that can help you feel safer.

4. Notice what steps you may take to further develop any resources. Key 6 may help you to refine your steps and make them manageable.

Self-Talk	Resources I Have Now That I Did Not Have Then	Resources That I Want to Develop	Things That Might Help Build These Resources
I should have fought back.	*I am a strong, tall adult now.*	*I would like to feel stronger. Go to self-defense class.*	*Doing strengthening exercises. (See Key 7.)*
I should have shouted for help.	*My voice is louder—just ask my children!*	*I would like to be able to stay present so that I can manage my overwhelm and make good choices about my safety.*	*Developing resources that help me to stay calm (see Key 4), to recognize triggers so that I am better prepared and able to distinguish memories of danger from what is happening in the present.*
It is all my fault; if only I had walked a different route.	*As an adult I have more control of my journeys and am more able to choose ways of traveling and routes where I feel safest.* *As an adult, I now have a cell phone and money. I am now able to call a cab if I feel unsafe.*	*No extra resource needed. I am an adult and this is a potent resource in itself.*	

Self-Talk	Resources I Have Now That I Did Not Have Then	Resources That I Want to Develop	Things That Might Help Build These Resources

FORGIVE-YOUR-LIMITATIONS MANTRA

It is possible for negative self-talk to return, as the fact of your past limitations might take a while to sink in deeply. Regular reviewing of your learning in this chapter may help.

Additionally, a mantra, sometimes called an affirmation, can be helpful. A mantra is a simple statement that you accept to be true, repeated to yourself either in your mind or aloud. The word *man-tra* translated from Sanskrit means "protect the mind." A mantra "talks over" the contrary belief and eventually overpowers it. Naming your own mantra is *not* a religious practice and can be used no matter your culture or religion.

1. Read the examples of mantras or affirmations.
2. Use your Mindful Gauge to determine whether any of those resonate with you. If not, or in addition, add others you have heard or that you make up just for yourself.

    It is important that there be a part of you that believes the mantra to be true so that you do not feel that you are in an argument with yourself when you use it, and so that it feels meaningful.
3. Write them out and put them in your pocket or purse, on your mirror, on your refrigerator, anywhere where a reminder would be helpful.

I did not choose what happened.	Recovery is not linear or time limited.
I am not what happened to me.	Recovery can be difficult. I am allowed to rest.
I am worthy of having needs and support.	I have the right to say no and to say yes.
Just like everything in nature, I belong.	It was not my fault.

FORGIVE-YOUR-LIMITATIONS LETTER

1. Read what you have written about your trauma response and your limitations in the earlier exercises.

2. If it helps to increase your self-compassion, imagine that a dear friend of the same age that you were at the time of the trauma held themselves accountable for what happened to them.

3. Write a letter to yourself forgiving your limitations at the time of the trauma. Include what you know about the science regarding your response to the trauma, as well as other limitations. You may want to include forgiveness for additional parts of the trauma you have been holding on to, such as:

   • surviving if others did not
   • severing ties with people that connected you to the trauma
   • focusing on your needs to survive and cope
   • not being able to help or rescue another to survive
     It might feel difficult to know where to start. Maybe just start with "I forgive me for . . ." This might be something you revisit through your recovery as you gain deeper acceptance and understanding.

4. Identify whether there is someone that you could share and discuss this with, perhaps a friend or a therapist.

Write your letter here:

KEY 5B RECONCILE FORGIVENESS AND SHAME

Share Your Shame

In Key 5, Part A we discussed the fact that trauma does not happen when one is in control of circumstances. As a result, it is common for those who have survived trauma to do all that they can to regain a sense of control, even at the cost of their relationship with themselves. It is in this way that trauma can lead an innocent victim to believe that the trauma was their fault, concluding, perhaps, that they are intrinsically bad or that there is something wrong with them and that this is why the trauma happened to them. Another version on this same theme is that a traumatic event can also lead some people to feel that the trauma has left them damaged as a person, as though experiencing trauma makes them less-than. Unfortunately, there are also some cultures and family systems that believe this, making it even more difficult for a trauma survivor to overcome and resolve feelings of shame.

Carla, from Key 5A, came to believe that she was a bad mother for not being able to do more when she and her terrified children were waiting for firefighters in the upstairs bedroom. Once she had accepted her limitations during the trauma, she was able to forgive herself, though some feeling of shame remained. Nonetheless, she felt more able to interact with others, and she joined a women's group where she met another mother who became a supportive friend. Using her Mindful Gauge to assess her decision, Carla chose to share her feelings of shame about what had happened. Her friend listened and asked Carla how she could support her. Carla had been worried that people would be horrified by her actions and share her shameful belief that she should have done more. To the contrary, her new friend's supportive reaction helped Carla's feelings of shame to dissipate.

WHAT IS THE POINT OF SHAME?

Though no one enjoys the feeling of shame, like all other emotions it serves a purpose; it is integral to our survival. Shame has enabled humans to survive in groups (tribes, families, communities, countries) by shaping behavior that benefits everyone. Shame alerts us that something is wrong, usually involving a social interaction and belonging.

Some animals also feel shame. A mother wolf is eating a bone when one of her puppies ventures closer to have an uninvited bite. The mother growls and the puppy runs, hiding its face with its paw in shame. After some time, the mother dog makes eye contact and the puppy comes out of hiding. Sometime later, the mother wolf leaves the bone for the youngsters to enjoy freely. The puppy learns that if it wants to remain part of the pack it must wait until it is invited to eat. Without shame, the puppy may have continued to push its luck, resulting in a longer-term, or even permanent, exile.

It is normal for parents to shape the behavior of their children, consciously or unconsciously, with shame. We have all experienced it growing up in our families, at school, and in social groups. Usually, it is just a normal part of growing up and helps us get along in various situations. Anticipating a feeling of shame can help someone to avoid doing something that would cause them to be called out or isolated. Problems with shame arise when, following an episode of rejection, reconnection does not occur. For example, if the mother wolf had continued to ignore the puppy, proper socialization would not have been possible. Shame usually guides people against decisions that, as with many social conventions, would be detrimental evolutionarily, such as incest.

On the other hand, *shamelessness* is another, somewhat underrecognized, problem of shame. When someone is not able to feel shame, they do not develop an internal guide for acceptable behavior. People who commit crimes to property and other people are often unable to feel shame. If you have experienced bullying or physical or sexual assault, you will have personally known the cost of shamelessness.

1. Recall a time when you have benefited from shame. Shame has likely helped you numerous times to fit in with your family, community, and network. In addition, perhaps shame has helped you to make a positive decision or more beneficial choices. For example, Sally felt ashamed when she ate her husband's birthday chocolates without asking first. Disliking that feeling of shame, she bought more to replace them. Monty impulsively stole some longed-for sunglasses at a store, but the shame he felt helped him to put them back before he was caught.

    If you feel comfortable doing so, write a memory of shame being useful to you. If you do not want to write it down, just use a few minutes now to remember it:

2. Circle the ways that shame has helped you. Add others to the boxes.

Signaled that I had overstepped a friend's boundaries (or was about to)	Motivated the repair of a relationship	Prevented social rejection	Stopped me from breaking the law
Helped me to be accountable	Helped me make decisions	Interrupted me from pursuing an affair	

3. As you recall the beneficial aspect of shame, notice whether you can remember what helped the shame to dissipate. Below are some strategies that others have used to dissipate feelings of shame. They may or may not be representative of your experience. Circle any that are and write in others that you think of.

Taking appropriate responsibility	Planning a way to do it differently next time	Reconnecting with my body (using movement or self-care, etc.)	Apologizing
Reflecting on and reassessing my values	Shifting to think of the behavior or action as problematic, rather than myself as the problem		

HOW DO YOU KNOW WHEN YOU FEEL SHAME?

It can be useful to be able to distinguish shame from other emotions, particularly how it feels for you. Once you recognize it, you may be more easily able to evaluate your particular situation. For example, you might be surprised to learn that a very relevant question could be: Is the shame you are feeling actually your shame? Sometimes, as will be discussed below, a trauma victim may adopt feelings of shame that rightfully belongs with someone else, one whose shamelessness allowed them to perpetrate trauma, or another who did not prevent a trauma when they possibly could have.

Do you notice any change in . . . ?

Sensations in your body?

Draw or write if you feel a change in sensation in your body when you feel shame. Maybe you feel hot, cold, tingling, butterflies, legs want to run, hands want to hide you face. Then do the same with the other characteristics listed to the right.

Thoughts:

Images in your mind:

Mood:

Behavior/actions:

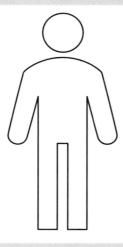

Does your shame have a message for you?
For example, I am afraid I will not be liked; I am worried that people will think badly of me.

RELIEVE YOUR SHAME

Many people who have experienced trauma take on much more shame and responsibility for what happened than is equitable.

Carla felt ashamed that she did not predict the apartment fire even though there was no way she could have. The fire was electrical, and nothing had been flagged in the recent safety check. Moreover, it did not even start in her apartment, but in one of those below hers. Though she wished there was more she could have done while she waited for help, there was not. Exploring the facts of what happened helped her to accept that she had been feeling shame for something that was completely out of her control.

What causes you to feel shame about the trauma you experienced?	The part of the traumatic incident that I was in control of
I was raped and I froze, I did not scream or run away.	*None.*
I got bumped into at a gathering. It reminded me of being attacked and I reacted defensively.	*Though the thinking part of my brain was not engaged, I now know the person who bumped into me did not try to attack me. I can take responsibility and apologize.*
I should have known the earthquake was going to happen and gotten to safety.	*None.*

HEALTHY SHAME VERSUS SHAMELESSNESS

As discussed earlier in this Key, shame is essential to our maintaining morality and ethics and passing those on to the next generation. It is thought that traumas that have been committed purposely by another are often perpetrated by those who do not have a healthy amount of shame. Though no one really knows how it happens, it is quite usual for someone who is victimized by a shameless perpetrator to take on (what should be) that person's shame. That is why, in part, a victim of rape often feels very ashamed for having been raped.

And, of course, it does not help when cultural or societal beliefs additionally condemn trauma survivors rather than the perpetrators.

My nervous system automatically in control during the traumatic incident	The part of the traumatic incident that someone else was in control of	The part of the traumatic incident that was beyond anyone's control
I believed my life was in danger. The thinking part of my brain was not available.	*The rapist was responsible for the rape.*	
The emotional part of my brain believed I was in the same danger as before and reacted in fight mode. The thinking part of my brain was not available.	*Even though it was an accident, I should not have gotten bumped at the gathering.*	
My amygdala chose the freeze response because we were trapped. There was no safe path.	*No one predicted it.*	*Earthquakes are unpredictable.*

PUT SHAME BACK WHERE IT BELONGS

Depending on the type of trauma you experienced, the table in the previous exercise may indicate that some of the shame you are feeling, or have felt, actually belongs with someone else.

In this exercise, we explore multiple creative ways to symbolically send shame back to whomever it actually belongs to. You might like to create a ritual, write a letter, burn an effigy, and so on, to represent your sending the shame back. You will find ideas for this at the end of this section. Choose or create the method that resonates most with you.

WRITING

1. Write a story about how it would have been different if the person who hurt you had been able to feel shame instead of having been shameless.
2. Draft a letter in your imagination or on paper to that person telling them that the shame for what happened is theirs. (Caveat: We do **not** recommend that you actually **send** such a letter.)

   Write a supportive letter to the part of you who feels ashamed, explaining which portion of shame is healthy for that part (i.e., it is good you know what was wrong so you will not be repeating behaviors or carrying forward what a perpetrator did) and which portions do not belong to that (or any) part of you (i.e., shameless perpetrators are 100% responsible for what they do).
3. Read through the suggested rituals at the end of this exercise to judge whether you would like to choose one to send back the shame.

DRAWING AND PAINTING

1. Read your entries in the previous table where someone else's shamelessness was responsible for your trauma.
2. Use your Mindful Gauge to notice whether you continue to feel any of that shame.
3. Choose colors that represent that feeling. Use your Mindful Gauge to check which colors feel "right."

4. Make marks on the paper. Follow your instinct to make marks in the way that feels right. Maybe long lines up and down, or swooping curves from side to side. Maybe hard dots or splotches.

5. As you paint or draw, imagine the shame leaving your mind and body. For example, imagine the shame going from your hand into the paintbrush or pencil and coming out onto the paper.

6. You may also wish to add the mantra from the previous exercise.

7. Read through the suggested rituals at the end of this exercise to judge whether you would like to choose one to send back the shame.

COLLAGE

1. Cut out images from magazines, newspapers, and catalogs that represent the shame you have been holding for the other person and wish to let go of.

2. Create a collage using the images. Maybe include words or use cut-out letters or include a mantra.

3. Read through the suggested rituals at the end of this exercise to judge whether you would like to choose one to send back the shame.

CLAY

1. Use air-drying clay from a craft store, Play-Doh, natural clay, or one you make yourself from flour, water, salt, and food coloring. Shape it in different ways that feel good or satisfying to you, maybe pounding it with your fists, pinching it between your fingers, squeezing it hard, flattening it, and so on.

2. Next, mold it into a shape that represents the shame you have been holding that is not yours. It may be a simple shape or it might turn into a creature or an object that is a metaphor or symbol of that shame.

3. Consider whether you would like to add paint.

4. Read through the suggested rituals at the end of this exercise to judge whether you would like to choose one to send back the shame.

Put your creation in a fireplace and watch it be consumed by the flames and go up in smoke.	Fold your artwork into the shape of a boat and drop it into a river, or put the clay object onto a makeshift "raft" of sticks or leaves and let it float away.
Tear the paper up into tiny pieces.	Put your creation somewhere special as a reminder that the shame is not yours.
Smash the clay or tear up the pieces of paper and bury them.	

SINGING

1. Listen to and read the lyrics of a song, or songs, that resonates with the feeling of handing back the shame or a feeling of being free from the shame that should belong to someone else.

    The table below offers some suggestions of songs that have given us that feeling.

    Of course, song lyrics and music can be incredibly powerful and have different messages for different people. Therefore, the songs listed here are only suggestions. They may elicit a different, even unhelpful, response for you.

    Use your Mindful Gauge to choose songs that make sense to or speak to you.

    Add your own songs here and then circle any that appeal to you for helping to send shame to where it belongs.

"Mean"—Taylor Swift	"Roar"—Katy Perry
"This Is Me"—Keala Settle and The Greatest Showman Ensemble	"I'm Still Standing"—Elton John
"I Am What I Am"—Gloria Gaynor	"Step by Step"—Whitney Houston
"Back in My Body"—Maggie Rogers	"I'm Coming Out"—Diana Ross
"Survivor"—Destiny's Child	"Strong Enough"—Cher
"Don't Stop"— Fleetwood Mac	"Born to Fight"—Tracy Chapman

"Brave"—Sara Bareilles	"No Scrubs"—TLC
"I Will Survive"—Gloria Gaynor	"Feeling Good"—Nina Simone
"(Something Inside) So Strong"—Labi Siffre	"Numb"—Sylvan Esso

2. You may choose to simply listen, sing by yourself, or sing along with a recording of a song. Whether singing or listening, notice how the song feels to you. When singing with a recording, notice the feeling of your voices connecting. Some people like to listen to songs with many voices, such as groups or choirs, as though they have a whole team of people singing with them. See if you would like to try that.

3. As you sing you might imagine the shame leaving your body and mind through the song and your exhale.

DANCING

Those of you who enjoy dancing may wish to dance to a song that resonates with the feeling of letting go of the shame that belongs to another, allowing your body to move with the music, releasing the shame as you move. The songs in the singing exercise might be appropriate, or use another that you have noticed has generated this feeling. Add to the list any you find useful. Shaking, wriggling, and other ways of moving can be great ways to release long-held feelings. We shall explore this further in Key 7.

SHARE YOUR SHAME TO CONNECT
OR RECONNECT WITH OTHERS

Trauma, particularly sexual and physical abuse, holds an underlying stigma in many societies that can result in not being believed and in further shame from being shunned. The Me Too movement, which began around 2006, made possible the uncovering of many people's traumas that had previously been disbelieved by families, police, courts, and so on. Though the risk of isolation from shame is still present, the Me Too movement has made it possible for many victims to come forward and get support.

Kimi avoided her friends because she was ashamed of her trauma symptoms. She worried about whether she would have a panic attack or flashback while in a social situation. She realized she needed to improve her ability to cope with the fact of her trauma. As a result, she carefully selected a good therapist she felt was a good fit for her. With the help of therapy Kimi developed more control of her flashbacks, identified her triggers, and gained a variety of tools to help her feel calmer. Once she had identified what helped, she was increasingly more confident at letting others know her needs.

Though Kimi felt more in control, she still felt ashamed about how she had treated her friends in the early days of her recovery. This shame highlighted her desire for reconnection.

A common feature of shame is an impulse to withdraw or a feeling of exile. As such, it is often remedied only by an experience and feeling of connection. Humans, just like the wolf pups mentioned in the previous section, also heal shame in connection with others.

Connecting with others to heal shame will be difficult for just about anyone. However, for those who grew up isolated because of experiencing trauma in their homes, it may be even more difficult. Nonetheless, it is possible to carefully choose one or more friends or family members to connect with, including sharing personal shame. However, patience is necessary, as it is not an easy process for either the one who feels isolated by shame or the one who wants to be there to connect and help heal.

Sharing your shame should be well considered both for healing and to avoid further isolation and disconnection. It will likely involve several steps.

Kimi's first attempt at talking to a friend was not successful. The friend brought her young daughter to their meeting in the park and was distracted. Kimi realized that to get her needs met she would need a better plan, to prepare both herself and her friend so that their eventual conversation would help them to connect with each other without distractions.

For her second attempt, Kimi used her Mindful Gauge to choose a friend who, when Kimi imagined telling her, brought her a feeling of calm. Kimi had previously experienced her to be compassionate and a good listener, and to have reasonable boundaries. She felt that exploring her shame with this friend might help her to feel less alone in those feelings and able to consider reconnecting with the rest of her friends.

Kimi used her Mindful Gauge to identify where a good place to meet would be. She decided she would cook a meal for them both at her place. And they planned a time when her friend could come without any of her children or anyone else and give her full attention to Kimi.

Kimi explained that she had something important and sensitive that she would like to talk about and so it would be great if they could meet somewhere quiet and to make sure they both had enough time so as not to feel rushed. She said that she wanted to share with her something she was feeling shame about, and asked if that would be okay. Her friend explained that she had a busy week but was free Sunday evening and would also feel more emotionally available then. Kimi felt comforted that her friend had been honest about her availability.

When her friend arrived, Kimi checked in again about whether her friend still had time to stay awhile and talk. Kimi shared that she wanted the friend to listen, and maybe share her own experience of shame. She hoped to feel less alone in this feeling. Kimi explained that she did not feel comfortable with long hugs or physical contact at the moment.

Before dinner, Kimi told her friend about the shame she had felt. Her friend listened, and even shared one of her own experiences of feeling shame. Kimi felt a warm sense of connection.

A little like with other challenging and stressful life experiences, such as death and terminal illness, many people can shy away from hearing about traumatic experiences and feelings of shame. Many feel inadequately prepared or equipped to respond in a way that is helpful. You might have noticed someone changing the subject, minimizing, or brushing off your concern. Often such responses are indicative not of your importance to them but, rather, of their own discomfort or lack of understanding and experience. In their distress, many become awkward and say and do things that feel uncompassionate or can unintentionally increase the shame felt by the survivor. Choosing the right person and right time and laying some foundation can be essential to successfully sharing your shame.

As it was for Kimi, it is important to consider carefully the different elements of sharing your shame. Using your Mindful Gauge to determine the person, place, and time can be useful. Asking your friend whether they feel comfortable with your sharing something difficult can help to prepare them and, depending on how they respond to that question, may alert you to whether this is the right person right now.

Decide in advance how much of your trauma story you wish to share. If your goal is to share your shame, it may not be necessary to share any of that story at all. But if you feel that it is a part of sharing your shame, be sure that, as advised in Key 3, you do not share intricate details of your trauma. That would be unhelpful and unnecessary, particularly when talking with friends and family. Instead, it may be useful to share a very brief outline, headlines only, **no details**. Or even just the fact of it and no more: "I was raped." "I survived a tsunami." "My parent was violent." And so on.

Write a list of some of the things you are feeling ashamed of. Do not overwhelm yourself by trying to list them all.

1. Next, order them 1–10, 10 being the thing that brings you the most feelings of shame, 1 being the least.

1–10	Things I am feeling ashamed about

2. Read the statement that you feel least shame about and pay attention to how you feel. Feel free to change your statement in any way.
3. Write the names of the possibilities of people (or one person) whom you feel you might like to share this shame with. Using the questions below with your Mindful Gauge may help you to work out who is the right choice. Be alert that your Mindful Gauge might tell you that there is not a right choice at the moment and that this is something to revisit at a later date.

   The possible people (or person) that you want to share with might include a trusted family member or close friend. Or perhaps there might not be anyone currently in your life that you feel would be a good candidate for this exercise. You can always return to this or any exercise in the future. Alternatively, you might wish to try it out first with a beloved pet to gauge how it feels saying your feelings aloud. Animals tend to be great listeners and comforters.

Names or name of possible people or person to share with:

| 1 | 2 | 3 | 4 |

4. Notice whether each of the people you have chosen has the qualities you would like in a person to share your shame with. Reflect on your experiences with this person and, in the table below, put a check or a cross in the number box corresponding with the person listed above. Use your Mindful Gauge to help. Add any qualities that are important to you in this process, or strike out any that are not. As no one is perfect, aim for someone who is "good enough" to share your shame with.

   (Caveat: You may find that you do not currently know anyone that feels right. If so, consider whether that means you are not ready to share your shame, whether you need to add to your current network, or whether you need to talk more with one or more of the people you might consider to establish how well they fit your requirements.)

Do they . . .	1	2	3	4
Listen without judgment or making it about them?				
Respect your boundaries?				
Encourage you without pressuring you?				
Demonstrate the ability to self-regulate their own feelings and nervous system?				
Hold their own boundaries?				
Give you a feeling of safety or calm?				
Allow space for you to show and share your feelings?				

5. How would you like someone to respond when you share your shame?

Imagine talking with each of the people listed. You might like them to simply listen, or you might want their more active support to your sharing, or something in between. What, if anything, do you want them to say and do?

> Say to you (e.g., just listen/ "I have felt shame too and struggle with it"/"Let me know how I can help"/"Let us think of an action plan to help")

> What would you not like them to say or do?
> (e.g., physical touch: give you a hug/show their feelings if they are upset)

Consider what it would be like to share with your friend how you hope they will react. Remember that no one is likely to be able to guess what you need from them. Everyone is different. For example, how Kimi hoped her friend would respond may be very different from your own needs. What do you need to feel comfortable to share your shame? Or, if you do not feel comfortable to share it, consider whether that is because you need more inner support or more outer support. And remember, if you are not used to doing this, the first time is always the hardest. You will have a better chance of getting your needs met if they are known. Once a friend knows what you want, they can consider whether it is something they are able to give. Also consider that they may not be able to. Remember: Friends cannot always give each other what they need. That does not mean they are not quality friends, only that everyone has limitations.

6. Now, using the previous answers, write a script including
   • what you are feeling ashamed about;

- the boundaries you would like to hold in the conversation. These include how you would like and not like your friend to respond physically and verbally; and
- what you hope to hear or gain from the conversation.

Read the example, then write a script of what *you* would like to say in the blank space below.

As explored in Key 3, you *do not* need to tell them the details of your shame or trauma. In fact, we advise against it. You may simply wish to state that you have been struggling.

Kimi

Thank you for meeting me. I would very much like it if you were able to listen to how I have been experiencing a lot of shame recently. If you feel comfortable, when I have told you how I have been feeling, I would welcome you to share something of your own experience of shame. I feel that it would help to know that I am not alone in feeling this difficult emotion.

I do not feel comfortable with long hugs or most physical contact at the moment, but if it feels okay for you, I would like you to touch or hold my hand as I tell you.

I have been feeling shame about not being in contact with my friends. I have found it difficult to be in large groups and busy places recently. As a result, I ignored their calls and messages to avoid talking about why I did not want to meet; and now the shame about ignoring them prevents me from reconnecting.

Another example:

I have been feeling a lot of shame because I was molested some years ago. I believed that it was because there was something wrong with me that I was targeted. And I feel ashamed and dirty that I was treated like that. I do not want to tell you the details, but I wanted you to know so you would not take it personally if I reject your touching me sometimes. Have you ever felt any kind of shame like that?

---

7. Imagine each of the people you have listed responding in the way you hope. Does this feel realistic? Then use your Mindful Gauge (from Key 1) to predict your response to sharing with each of the people. Which, if any, of the people are most likely to respond in a way that you would like them to?

   If any of them seem good prospects, use your Mindful Gauge to work out the most appropriate time and location to ask them about meeting so you can share with them.

8. Then, following a meeting with one of your chosen people, evaluate how it went. Would you share with them again? If so, why? If not, why not?

BE ACCOUNTABLE AND
COMPASSIONATE WITH YOURSELF

If criticism were curative, the whole world would be well.
—DENTON L. ROBERTS and FRANCES THRONSON, *Able and Equal*

Following a trauma, you may have said things or reacted in ways that you feel ashamed about. As discussed in Key 4, the feelings of overwhelm and feeling out of control can continue in the aftermath of trauma. It is not unusual for someone reeling or recovering from trauma to be (what others might perceive as) inappropriate at times. If that has happened, it can be a good idea to touch base with anyone you might have offended and apologize. At the same time, be gentle with yourself, because it is easy to make mistakes in relationships when one has recently been hurt themselves.

Jack, a lieutenant in the army, was recently back from a war zone, having dinner with his friends back in his home town. He was leaving the restaurant when he suddenly felt a hand on his shoulder. He immediately flipped his lid as his fight response automatically activated. He spun around and nearly punched his friend in the face before recognizing who it was. Seconds later, when the thinking part of his brain came back online, lid back in place, he realized it was his friend Brent, bringing him the wallet he had accidentally left behind.

Jack was mortified. He felt that he should have better control of his reactions and felt terrible about coming so close to actually hurting his friend. After that he avoided meeting up with friends, feeling incredibly ashamed about what had happened and worried he could not be trusted.

Instead of reaching out for help to manage such triggers, Jack spent the rest of his time on leave at his parents' house, declining offers of hanging out with his friends. He worried that he was a bad and dangerous person.

Jack was recovering from trauma and in that recovery period his survival system was likely on high alert, for fear of the trauma reoccurring.

Though his actions had emotional or physical repercussions on people he cared about, where the blame for his actions lie can be blurred. Jack would never have nearly hit his friend if he had not been traumatized. Even though his actions are trauma related, taking responsibility for them is important (including getting help to increase his ability to stop impulses to violence)—for healing from trauma, maintaining relationships that are important to him, and helping to bring resolution to his feelings of shame.

1. In the box below, write the ways that you have coped or reacted since the trauma that you feel okay about, or even proud of. These might include: "Continuing to look after a child or a pet"; or "Remembered a friend's birthday"; or "Asked for help when I needed it"; or "Bought this book to start to take charge."

Ways I have coped or reacted since the trauma that I feel okay about or, even, am proud of:

2. Make a list of ways that you have coped or reacted since the trauma that you feel guilty or ashamed about.

   Then, number them 1 to 10, with 10 being the one that you find most difficult, and 1 being the one you find least difficult.

1–10	Ways I have coped or reacted since the trauma that I feel guilty or ashamed about:

3. Notice, and write down, your beliefs about those reactions.

   Take note that it was nearly punching his friend that made Jack think of himself as bad, dangerous, and not to be trusted. However, it was this specific reaction rather than his whole being that was problematic.

   In the Belief About the Action column, rewrite any beliefs that you hold that refer to your whole being, changing them to refer to the behavior, as in the example.

   Notice how changing the sentence retains the responsibility and control of the problematic behavior, while also showing compassion for yourself.

Belief about my whole self	Belief about the action
I lashed out when I was scared because I am a dangerous person.	*I lashed out when I was scared. That behavior is not okay and I can learn to contain it.*
I ignored my friends because I am a rude and selfish person.	*I ignored my friends because I was overwhelmed. When I am less overwhelmed, I will be able to be with my friends again with ease.*

Jack avoided Brent after the incident because he was afraid that Brent would confirm Jack's fears that Brent no longer wanted a relationship. Though apologizing was difficult, when Jack explained, Brent had a better understanding of what happened between them and they were able to reconcile.

4. Reconnect and make amends. You may wish to apologize directly to someone that you feel you have hurt while you have been coping. Use the numbering system to identify those who will be easiest to start with.

5. Start with the incident you feel least worried or ashamed about.

Key Review

Did you remember to use your Mindful Gauge to evaluate the exercises in this chapter? If not, was that by choice or because you forgot?

	Did this exercise help, or make you feel worse?	If it helped, what reaction did you have that told you it helped? (For example, felt calmer or stronger or more present.)
Autonomic Nervous System Response		
Trauma-Response Limitations		
Additional Limitations		
Should Have, Would Have, Could Have		
Shall, Will, Can Resources		
Forgive-Your-Limitations Mantra		

If you forgot, consider whether you want to go back and do that.
Once you have completed an exercise you may wish to jot down your response and its effectiveness for you in the table.

If it helped, could it be adapted to help more? How?	If it helped, when do you plan to use it?	If it did not help, could you change or adapt it to better suit you? How?

	Did this exercise help, or make you feel worse?	If it helped, what reaction did you have that told you it helped? (For example, felt calmer or stronger or more present.)
Forgive-Your-Limitations Letter		
What Is the Point of Shame?		
How Do You Know When You Feel Shame?		
Relieve Your Shame		
Put Shame Back Where It Belongs		
Share Your Shame to Connect or Reconnect With Others		
Be Accountable and Compassionate With Yourself		

If it helped, could it be adapted to help more? How?	If it helped, when do you plan to use it?	If it did not help, could you change or adapt it to better suit you? How?

KEY 6 TAKE SMALLER STEPS FOR BIGGER LEAPS

Little by little, the bird makes its nest.
—ERIC V. COPAGE, *Black Pearls*

As I (author, Babette), am sitting at my computer working on this manuscript, the distance from my chair to my front door is approximately 10 feet (three meters). If I set a goal is to reach that door, how do I do that?

- If I try to get there in one big leap, I am not likely to make it and probably will also hurt myself in the effort.
- If I try to get there in two very big steps, my stride likely will not be long enough so I will not make it, and also might hurt myself, strain something, by trying that.
- The same is possible if I attempt to do it in three steps.

So how can I guarantee reaching my goal of getting to the door without hurting myself? There is only one choice: *I must take smaller steps.* Actually, even if I walk the distance in four, five, six, seven, eight, or even more total steps, I will definitely get to the door. Using more steps may take me a little more time, but by doing so I can be sure that I do, indeed, get to the door, and without hurting myself.

Couch to 5K

Couch to 5K is a popular guided-running app in the United Kingdom. It provides a series of audio recordings that guide the user through a 9-week (63-day) exercise program. Day 1 starts with mainly walking and the occasional short jog. Over the 9 weeks, the amount of actual running is increased little by little until the app user is running for 3 miles (5 kilometers) several times a week.

Of course, it would be ridiculous to expect someone who rarely exercises to run a marathon. Even if they tried, they would become exhausted, their muscles would not be strong enough and, also important, they would be setting themselves up to fail. If a new runner wanted to run a marathon, then attempting the whole 26 miles on their first outing would not only result in failure, but the damage they would do to themselves could set them back months or years in achieving any kind of exercise goal. The same principle applies to trauma recovery; large goals are best achieved through a series of small and achievable steps.

Facing the enormity of achieving a goal can feel overwhelming. However, breaking the goal down into manageable chunks and focusing on what small bit is possible *right now* not only helps to start the process but also helps to keep it going. If any nonrunner believed they had to achieve the goal of a 3-mile run on the first try, they would likely feel so overwhelmed that they would not even put on their sneakers. Whereas if they think in terms of taking one small step at a time (pun intended), they might first put on their sneakers and walk for a minute or two today. Tomorrow they could walk for a few more minutes and jog a few steps. The next day, they might walk again and add a slightly longer (but still short) jog. That way, over time, they will achieve their goal.

SOMETIMES AVOIDANCE IS A FRIEND

You may have heard friends, therapists, or books telling you that avoiding your feelings or trauma memories is a bad thing, and that you should face your fears head-on. However, if you have read the previous Keys in this book, you will know that we do not agree. At times, avoidance—permanently or for a limited time—can be just the right strategy for recovery.

In her spare time, Vanessa enjoys rock climbing. Until recently most of the rock climbing she had done involved a single climb up a particular smaller crag. Her eventual goal was to rock-climb the whole mountain. However, despite her training for this big challenge over time, even the idea of it still made her anxious.

When Vanessa arrived at the foot of the mountain for the big climb she had been slowly working toward, and her eyes ran from the base to the summit, she felt very nervous. However, she remembered that she could split the climb into smaller steps. For that day she decided:

- First step: She put her coat on. Her attention was sometimes drawn back to look at the summit and she felt nervous again, but when she attended to putting one arm in its coat sleeve, and then the other, and fastening the zipper, she felt calm.
- Step two: She put on her backpack, one strap and then the other.
- Further steps: She carried on like that throughout the day. Even on the face of the cliff she kept her focus on each subsequent tiny step, one at a time: Move right foot to the hole 8 inches higher than where it currently is, move right hand 6 inches to the right, and so on.

Identifying her climb as being made up of small steps rather than one big one meant that she was able to accomplish it without getting overwhelmed. The small steps also helped her to feel that it was okay to take breaks in between steps, rather than pushing through until the overarching goal was complete.

Avoiding a task, or finding alternate ways around it, until you are able to chip away at it piece by piece while staying calm and present, is much more beneficial to recovery than powering through regardless. Taking too big a step, or going too fast, can result in feeling much, much worse; in some cases, it can even be retraumatizing. It can also result in losing any desire to try again. Going at a pace that is right for you is essential to success and continued success. You can use your Mindful Gauge (Key 1) to determine the right pace for you, noting that your best pace might change from day to day. A person with a running goal might feel able to walk a few minutes more one day, and on another day might feel strong enough to run a few strides, but there will also be days where it is best to go slower and do less than the day before.

A colleague of ours, Michael Gavin, sometimes suggests considering a kind of pre-step "thinking about thinking about doing something." For some goals your Mindful Gauge might let you know that simply considering the goal is enough of a step right now.

There may be a part of you that wants to power through, to reach the end as fast as you can. Here we are reminded of Aesop's fable about the tortoise and the hare. When the hare ridicules the tortoise's slow pace, the tortoise challenges the hare to a race. The hare sets off at great speed, the tortoise ambling along at a speed comfortable to him. Believing that the race will be easily won, Hare takes a nap, only to find on waking that Tortoise has finished the race.

Going slowly and steadily does not mean that you will not achieve your goal. On the contrary, like Tortoise, you will get there, and it can be done at a pace that is comfortable, manageable, and safe, confident but not overconfident. Setting big goals and then feeling exasperated that you have not met them can be disheartening. By taking the approach of splitting a task into small steps, you have the opportunity for many celebrations along the way, which will help to build confidence and support your motivation. The new runner who does not manage to run 26 miles may see only a failure, but the new runner who runs their first half mile has something to celebrate, whether their eventual goal is 3 miles a day or a marathon.

Our modern culture is fast paced. There is a value put on getting things done as quickly as possible. You may find that doing things your way is a challenge; going slower than others may feel awkward or unusual to you. Giving yourself permission to take the time you need may feel selfish or as though you could be left behind. Keep in mind the tortoise and the hare. You will get there.

Though we encourage you to take small steps wherever possible, we appreciate that it might not be possible in every aspect of your life. You may also be reading this and worrying that there are some things you must do now, such as take care of children or animals or earn money. The exercises in this Key explore alternative and supportive steps that may help with these. For example, if a trauma happened at your workplace, you may decide to work from home for a while or find an interim job that causes you less distress. If you notice that a method of transport increases your distress, you may be able to use an alternative.

The exercises in this chapter offer ways to consider breaking goals down into smaller, doable steps. They will help you to take your time and make use of your Mindful Gauge to notice the right pace for you to stay calm, be in control, and be consistently taking steps to achieve your goals.

This is a reminder for you to use your Mindful Gauge with the exercises below. You might find the Mindful Gauge to be a handy tool for you. Alternatively, the idea of it might inspire you to an evaluation method of your own design.

First, check with your Mindful Gauge how it feels to read the exercise. If it feels okay, continue the exercise, and continue to check in. Then check your Mindful Gauge afterwards. Do you feel better or worse? Is this a good resource for you?

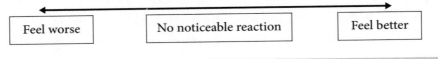

| Feel worse | No noticeable reaction | Feel better |

REDUCING TO SMALLER STEPS

Practicing reducing everyday tasks into tiny steps can help you to get into the habit. This first exercise may seem a little simple; however, it can be great to practice on an activity that is not so consequential, and does not trigger any concerns, before you apply the same principle to a more critical goal.

METHOD

1. Make a list of the steps needed to get from where you currently are sitting reading to the nearest door. Write it down.

   Right now, for me (author, Vanessa), these are:

   a. Push my chair back from my desk a little.
   b. Position myself ready to stand.
   c. Put my hands on the arms of the chair.
   d. Push with my hands and legs to stand up.
   e. Turn to face the door.
   f. Take seven steps to reach the door.

The procedure will differ depending on whether you are sitting or lying down right now, what kind of chair you are sitting in or surface you are lying on, whether you use a wheelchair or other support for mobility, whether you are at a desk or a table, and so on.

2. Next, look through your list and check whether any of the steps can be further broken down. For example, I could break down Point b from my original list, above, into:

   a. Put both my feet flat on the floor under my knees.
   b. Tip my weight forward a little.

3. Test it out: Follow your steps to reach the door. Did you miss anything?

4. Next, apply the same technique to three more tasks: washing dishes, making a drink, and washing your hands—or tasks you choose instead. You can use the following diagram for guidance.

There is space for nine steps in the diagram, but you might identify more steps or fewer. If you notice more, add them in.

1. Steps to get from where you are to the door

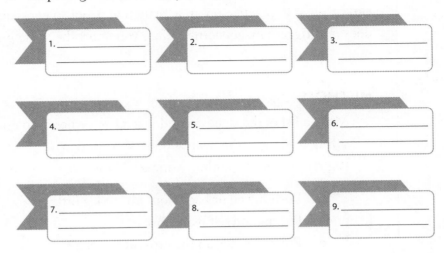

2. Steps to washing dishes

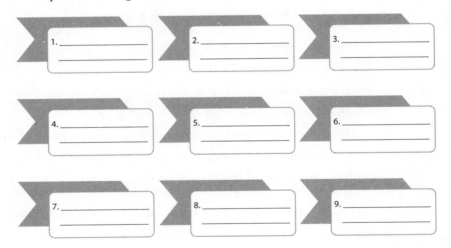

3. Steps to making a drink

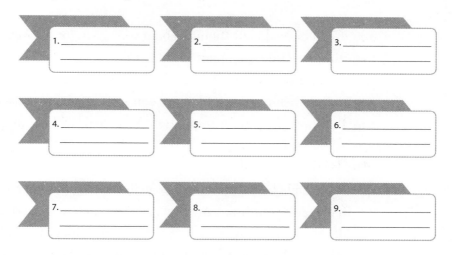

4. Steps to washing your hands

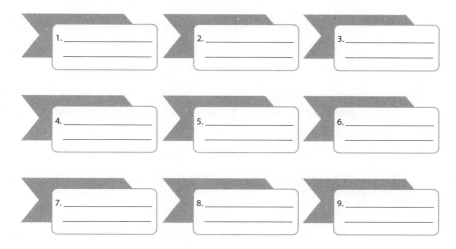

RECOVERY GOALS

You might have already thought about your goals for recovery, but if not, then this exercise is an opportunity to think about which recovery goals would improve your quality of life. Possibilities might include returning to work, helping a neighbor, (re)connecting with friends, or taking a trip. But those are just for inspiration. Your goals will be unique to you.

METHOD

1. In the table below, start a list of goals for your trauma recovery. Feel free to edit your list at any time, adding, subtracting, adjusting.
2. Identify how you will know that you have achieved a goal. For example, if you currently experience flashbacks, your goal might be to reduce their frequency or stop them quicker. Once you have achieved a goal you can always set another one.
3. Prioritize the goals, numbering them with 1 being the goal that is most urgent. Notice whether any goals are linked, with one goal needing to be achieved before another. For example, the goal of going on a road trip with friends may be achievable only once the goal of being a passenger while someone else drives has been achieved.
4. Once you have a beginning list, it will be possible for you to work with one at a time. See the following exercises.

Goal	How you know when you have achieved it	Priority (1–10)	Any goals that must be achieved before this one

SPLITTING ONE GOAL INTO STEPS

The task of completing one of your recovery goals may feel daunting. The trick is to keep splitting it down into smaller and smaller steps, until they are small enough for you to look at without distress and to easily achieve successfully. **Only attempt to work with one goal at a time**.

Here is an example: *Traveling to work one day, Vanessa's client, Paulo, was in a traffic accident. Though his physical injuries healed, he experienced many symptoms of PTSD, including flashbacks.*

Paulo's most urgent goal was returning to work. It was a job he enjoyed and, although his employers had been understanding, now that he was physically healed they were keen for him to return. However, Paulo was aware that if he did it too quickly, he could become retraumatized and end up more distressed, which, in turn, would end up with him taking even more time off.

He kept a flashbacks-trigger journal (Key 4) and noticed that the flashbacks got worse when he thought about going anywhere in his car, so a big step—driving to work—would be much too overwhelming.

Paulo knew he needed to make smaller steps but he found it difficult to think what the first step might be, until he cleverly realized he could figure this out backward. He started with his final goal of arriving at work. Then he continued to figure his steps backward like this:

- *arriving at work (the end goal)*
- *traveling to work*
- *leaving the house*
- *getting dressed for work*
- *getting up on time*
- *setting his alarm, the night before*
- *putting out his clothes for the morning*
- *making his lunch*
- *and so on . . .*

Working all the way back, he realized that the first step would be to speak to his boss and organize a shorter workday for the first week or two; he believed that would give him the space he needed to take the steps necessary to get him to work on time on his first day back.

METHOD

1. From your list of goals in the previous exercise, choose only one that feels *least* challenging. Success with something easier first will hopefully give you more confidence to figure out smaller steps and eventually to tackle the more difficult goals.

2. Break that goal down into small, manageable steps. Like Paulo, you may wish to work backward from the end goal.

3. Notice whether any of the steps could be several steps. The steps should be so tiny that you could accomplish one of them today. And also feel free to do steps out of order if that works as well or better for you.

4. Use your Mindful Gauge to make sure each of the steps is small enough.

Goal: _____

1
2
3
4
5
6
7
8
9
10

MANAGEABLE STEPS

Even once a goal is split into smaller steps, the steps themselves may feel daunting. When Paulo considered the first step, to call his boss, Gloria, he felt overwhelmed. Splitting that step down into even smaller steps meant that he could focus on each one at a time, without being overwhelmed by the bigger task. He further split the task of calling his boss, similarly to how you did with the everyday tasks in the first exercise of this chapter:

    a. write the points of what I want to say

    b. dial the number

    c. press the call button

    d. ask to speak to Gloria

    e. say hi

    f. read the points that I want to say

    g. listen to her response

    h. say goodbye

    i. hang up

One of Paulo's goals was to feel calm enough to drive to work, but whenever he thought about the journey he got overwhelmed. He used the previous exercise to take one step at a time. The first mini-step was to go outside and see the car. The first time he stepped outside and saw his car, he felt anxious. He used the mindfulness tools and resources (Key 1) that helped him to be calm and present. Keeping in mind that looking at the car was his task for today, and that he need not do any more, he succeeded in holding on to the calm feeling. He continued this for a week or so, until he could step outside and look at the car while staying calm the entire time.

The next step was to open the car door. He added this to the routine and, again, did this until he could go and open the door without feeling overwhelmed. The next step was to sit in the car with the door open.

Paulo continued in this way, moving to the next step only when he felt completely calm doing it. At times he felt frustrated with himself for not just getting in the car and driving away. He had days where he felt he had gone backward, and felt overwhelmed by steps that the day before had felt okay. However, he was able to be self-compassionate and focus on what he had already achieved: Only a few weeks earlier he had been unable to even look at the car, and now he was sitting inside it.

Like Paulo, you may take many weeks to accomplish the smaller steps in this exercise. Remember the story of the tortoise and the hare, and know that it is okay, and often much more beneficial long-term, to take it slow.

If you notice shame arising about the speed of your recovery it may be useful to revisit the exercises in Key 5 to support yourself.

METHOD

1. Choose one of the steps toward the goal that you felt was most difficult to achieve.
2. Split that step into even smaller steps.

3. Notice whether those mini-steps could be broken down even further. Use your Mindful Gauge to help notice whether a step is small enough, manageable enough to attempt today.

Step:_____

MINI-STEPS

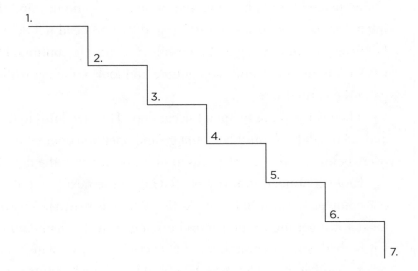

ALTERNATIVE STEPS

Often, when you are feeling overwhelmed, the part of the brain that helps you to think creatively closes down. Unfortunately, this means that you can miss alternative ways to solve a problem or reach a goal.

When faced with reaching the summit of a mountain, looking straight up at the rock faces and scree can make it feel impossible. However, taking a less direct route, zigzagging up like a sheep, will get you to the summit in a way that is much less strenuous and risky. Your chances of success will be greatly increased.

Paulo had been so overwhelmed by his desperation to return to work and his fear of driving there that he had not considered any alternatives. Below, Vanessa discusses her interventions:

I asked him whether it would be possible to do any parts of his job from home while he was taking the time to work through the steps toward feeling comfortable about driving. He was quiet for a moment and then laughed; he had not considered it. Though it would be difficult to do all aspects of his job at home, there were definitely some things that he could do. The next week he told me that his boss had agreed and was pleased that he would be back with the team, and was impressed by his creative thinking.

My initial suggestion opened the gate to other creative ways around his difficulty, including taking public transport and even sometimes walking to work.

There might be an alternative route to meeting your goal that provides easier steps. If you find a step that, even when reduced to many smaller steps, feels too difficult to tackle, then it may be worth considering what other path you could take. Sometimes, asking a trusted friend for help with this may offer a perspective you had not thought of.

METHOD

1. Notice whether one of the steps has a barrier that feels too difficult to overcome.

2. Add ideas to the boxes in the diagram that might offer an alternative solution to getting the same result, such as Paulo taking the bus to work.

3. Use your Mindful Gauge to choose which ones to try. Before you try them, imagine using them in that situation. Use your Mindful Gauge to notice whether you are ready to try it now, or whether you need a smaller step first.

Step:_____

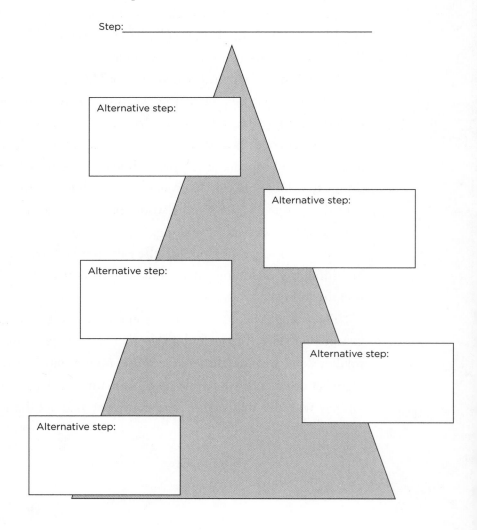

SUPPORTED STEPS

Carl's house was burgled when he was a teenager. He was at home alone that evening and woke in the night to the sound of heavy footsteps and people's voices that were not his mother's. Though the intruders did not enter his bedroom, it was terrifying for Carl, and since then he struggled with the dark. Whenever he slept alone, he became very anxious; every sound startled him and he would often lie awake listening for danger.

Carl's main recovery goal was to be able to sleep when his husband was working away from home. When he focused on the goal, he became overwhelmed; it felt impossible that he would ever succeed after all that time.

Inviting Carl to consider the alternatives, as well as resources that might support him, opened some possibilities. He thought that he might feel less alone if he had his phone next to him in bed and his partner agreed to have his phone on so that he could call him if he needed reassurance. He had previously felt that it would be childish to follow his impulse to check under the beds or to have a night-light, but he knew that these things would provide comfort.

He made a list of the steps he could take to find support and comfort, and used his Mindful Gauge to check whether each seemed like it would be more or less helpful. As a trial run, his husband agreed to spend a night in the spare room to simulate being away, but being near in case Carl needed him.

Before bedtime Carl carried out the steps he had identified, turning on the night-light, checking under the bed, and making sure his phone was nearby. The first night, he still listened for danger, but was able to stay calm. He became less embarrassed about taking these steps and they became part of his normal routine.

METHOD

1. Notice whether one of the steps in the Manageable Steps exercise has a barrier that feels difficult to overcome but for which there is not a clear alternative. For example, in Carl's case, there is not an alternative to sleeping.

2. Write the step in the center of the diagram and the resources to support you in the circles around it.
3. Test them out. Imagine yourself doing the step and having the support. Use your Mindful Gauge to assess whether the support helps you to feel better or worse.

Is there a way to test the resources as a practice, as Carl did with his husband sleeping in the next room instead of being away from home?

For example, if the step was to travel on public transport and your concern was about others around you, maybe a friend could travel with you and sit next to you at first. Then, once you were comfortable with that, they could sit in a different seat so that you could see them. And then, when you were ready, they could sit where you could not see them, and eventually you could try on your own.

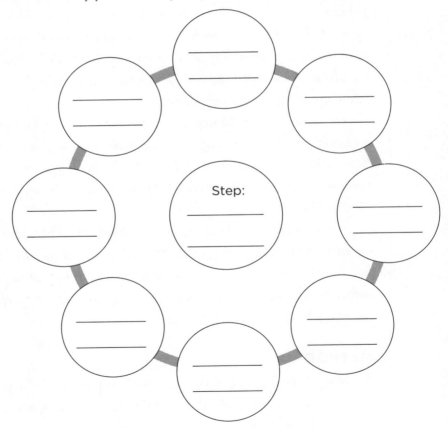

ADVOCATING YOUR PACE

Both authors of this book have experienced pressure from therapists and others to go at a faster pace than felt comfortable and safe for them. You, too, may experience this kind of pressure from your therapist, friends, family members, or colleagues. Their encouragement is likely to be well-meaning; they may wish for you to feel better or to be able to do the things you hope to do. However, such pressure is unlikely to be helpful.

You may need to advocate for yourself in these situations. When confronted you may feel overwhelmed, resulting in your mind feeling cloudy. Needing to defend yourself may feel difficult. Preparing stock replies may help with this. You might also wish to consider sharing this book with them, and specifically this Key, if you feel you would like extra backup.

Vanessa did exactly that with Babette's original 8 *Keys to Safe Trauma Recovery*. She was experiencing many symptoms of PTSD at the time, including flashbacks and panic attacks. The therapist she was seeing was very keen for her to talk about the trauma in her childhood. However, any reflection on that part of her life sent her symptoms into overdrive. Vanessa just wanted to feel safe and present.

Luckily, Vanessa had already read 8 *Keys to Safe Trauma Recovery* and knew she had the option to refuse to remember her trauma. At first, it was easier to say she did not want to that day. Another time, she told the therapist she felt that thinking about her past made her flashbacks worse and that she did not want to do it. In a later session, she took the 8 *Keys* book with her to therapy and told the therapist that she would rather not go into her history and that, according to the book, she did not have to.

Advocating for herself was not something she felt she should have to do, and there was some rupture in the therapeutic relationship that took a while to repair. However, by advocating for herself, Vanessa did gain a greater sense of ownership of her recovery and a powerful feeling of self-care. Once the boundaries had been agreed upon, she went on to have a long and productive relationship with that same therapist.

In the moment, when challenged, it can be difficult to know what to say. Preparing something in advance can help you to feel more assertive. You could rehearse saying the phrases, write them down so that you can read them if you need to, or hand them to anyone who challenges the pace of your recovery.

METHOD

1. Imagine being asked why you want to take your recovery at the pace that feels right for you.
2. Read the example reply and write some replies of your own. Practice saying them aloud. Use your Mindful Gauge to notice which feel easiest for you to say.
3. Imagine responding to a friend or therapist who you feel is pushing you. Use your Mindful Gauge to edit, rewrite, and practice your responses until you have a supply of ones that feel right for you.

4. Write them out on a piece of paper, your phone, or cards to carry with you. You might read them to yourself to remind you that it is okay to take the time you need; or you might hand them or read them aloud to the therapist or friend that challenges your pace.

> I can hear that you would like me to recover more quickly.
> This is the pace that feels right for me.

> When I think of the past trauma, I feel worse. I choose, instead, to go at a pace where I am able to maintain a feeling of safety and stability and focus on my resources.

> This is my therapy, not yours. It is likely you would need to do things differently than I do. Let us respect each other's needs and pace.

Key Review

Did you remember to use your Mindful Gauge to evaluate the exercises in this chapter? If not, was that by choice or because you forgot?

	Did this exercise help, or make you feel worse?	If it helped, what reaction did you have that told you it helped? (For example, felt calmer or stronger or more present.)
Reducing to Smaller Steps		
Recovery Goals		
Splitting One Goal Into Steps		
Manageable Steps		
Go Slow		
Alternative Steps		

If you forgot, consider whether you want to go back and do that.

Once you have completed an exercise you may wish to jot down your response and its effectiveness for you in the table.

If it helped, could it be adapted to help more? How?	If it helped, when do you plan to use it?	If it did not help, could you change or adapt it to better suit you? How?

	Did this exercise help, or make you feel worse?	If it helped, what reaction did you have that told you it helped? (For example, felt calmer or stronger or more present.)
Supported Steps		
Advocating Your Pace		

If it helped, could it be adapted to help more? How?	If it helped, when do you plan to use it?	If it did not help, could you change or adapt it to better suit you? How?

KEY 7 GET MOVING

> If you are in a bad mood, go for a walk. If you
> are still in a bad mood, go for another walk.
>
> —HIPPOCRATES

> Sweat every day. . . It's essential to circulate our
> energy, stay healthy, and release tension and feelings
> that are stored in every cell of our body.
>
> —THICH NHAT HANH, Twitter.com

In addition to the health benefits of physical exercise, there is a vast body of research that shows physical exercise has major benefits for mental well-being. Exercise increases

- serotonin, which helps to stabilize your mood;
- dopamine, which helps you to feel pleasure and motivation; and
- endorphins, which can reduce pain, help you to rest and sleep better, reduce irritability, and increase intuition and creative thinking.

When the response to trauma is to freeze, rather than fight or flee, the likelihood of PTSD is greater. Movement is central to antidoting the freeze response. Movement reinforces that the traumatic experience is over, and that now, in the present moment, you *can* move. Simply wiggling your fingers or looking around the room can break a freeze response and reinforce your epilogue (Key 3).

Overwhelming emotions can sometimes feel that they will spill out of you, as though your body is unable to contain them. Strength training is a great way to build a feeling of power, armor, protection, and of your body as a more secure container. However, everyone is different. So be sure to notice your own reactions and do only what leads you to feel more in control, calmer, and more present. A great way to be in charge is to notice what is and is not working for you.

Many trauma techniques promote relaxation in the form of lying down and gently releasing tension from your body. This can be beneficial for some people. However, for others, this kind of relaxation exercise can cause distress. Vanessa is a yoga teacher. She first started going to yoga classes while experiencing PTSD in her 20s. She enjoyed feeling strength in her body, being part of a group, and having a place she could go to that was quiet. However, whenever the yoga teacher invited them to lie down for guided relaxation, she felt anything but relaxed. She often felt as though she was about to have a panic attack, and had to use various distraction techniques to help her cope until that part of the class was over.

At home, she experimented with what helped her to feel calmer and more rested. She found that lying down often triggered a feeling of panic, but that sitting up or slowly walking was much more calming. She found that on most days, keeping her eyes open and slowly scanning the room was more calming than having her eyes closed. She also found that what was calming could change from day to day, so the process of experimenting became a part of her practice. Paying attention to her needs, and developing self-knowledge and self-acceptance, also gave her a feeling of calm.

When Vanessa became a yoga teacher, she encouraged her students, too, to be creative in exploring what felt right for them. She found that the biggest initial hurdle was for students to give themselves permission to meet their own needs, and to accept that what they found calming might not be what books, online videos, or even yoga teachers told them should be. You might discover the same. Just make sure to pay attention to what helps you, whether that is the same as you are told should help, is something completely different, or is some of each.

Many trauma survivors feel incredible fatigue. The symptoms of PTSD can be exhausting to manage, and many experience problems sleeping. Though it seems counterintuitive, exercising can increase energy and reduce fatigue. Not only are you more likely to sleep better if you have exercised, but exercising helps your body to better utilize the energy gained from nutrition. It can also help to reduce stress that might additionally be causing sleep difficulties.

Low-impact exercising is generally recommended when you experience fatigue. Swimming, cycling, walking, golf, and dance are low impact when practiced at a pace that best suits you. Take small steps (Key 5); use your Mindful Gauge (Key 1) to work out what is the right amount for you from one time to the next.

The first section of exercises for this Key is to support you in the practical elements to get you moving, such as creating good habits and choosing the right activities for you. The second section offers suggestions for movement activities that are intended to help you feel strong, present, and calm. Nonetheless, we encourage you to use your Mindful Gauge to assess which exercises are right for you.

With Others or Alone?

There is another factor to consider in identifying exercise that suits you best: Do you want to exercise with others or by yourself? Some activities can be done either in solitude or companioned (walking, hiking, yoga, and so on), while others can be done only together with others, for example, team sports. For many, a combination of both is optimal.

If you are someone who needs periods of alone time, by all means respect that. At the same time, you might also consider that one of the common consequences of trauma is a feeling of isolation. Activities with others can help with that. In addition, research is quite consistent that good contact and support can help to heal, and even to prevent, PTSD. Exercising with others can be a way to expand or strengthen your support network. And if you do not already have sources of support, it can be a way to start to build that into your life.

This is a reminder for you to use your Mindful Gauge with the exercises below. You might find the Mindful Gauge to be a handy tool for you. Alternatively, the idea of it might inspire you to an evaluation method of your own design.

First, check with your Mindful Gauge how it feels to read the exercise. If it feels okay, continue the exercise, and continue to check in. Then check your Mindful Gauge afterwards. Do you feel better or worse? Is this a good resource for you?

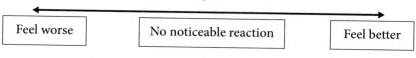

| Feel worse | No noticeable reaction | Feel better |

FIND YOUR ACTIVITY

The best way to engage in regular exercise is to find a type of exercise that you enjoy. Starting a new activity and maintaining it can be difficult. In this Key you will explore exercises to help with motivation; however, there will be nothing quite as motivating as finding fun, peace, or joy in the activity.

What kinds of physical activities did you enjoy when you were younger? Are there any that you would like to engage in now? An activity from your past may look and feel different now, but it can likely be adapted to your current abilities and lifestyle. For example, as a child, Rubi, from Key 4, loved riding her bike through forests, feeling the freedom of speeding down muddy hills. Now, she rides her bike to work, plotting enjoyable routes and providing an endorphin release that supports her throughout the day. She also avoids muddy hills on the commute so that she can arrive at work in a suitable condition.

METHOD

1. Notice whether there are one or two activities that have come to mind as you have read so far in this Key. If you have difficulty thinking of something, read the activities from the suggestions below to help you get ideas.

2. One at a time, imagine doing an activity. Use your Mindful Gauge to help you determine whether that would be something you would enjoy.

3. If it feels unachievable right now, notice how it might be adapted to suit you. Remember how the running program in Key 6 started with slow walks, gently building up to jogs until, after many weeks, the participant ran 3 miles.

4. Think about how feasible it would be to do this activity regularly, weighing up your time, the cost and equipment needed, and how accessible it would be for you. Kayaking might seem great, but if you live far away from water then it might be better to also choose something you can do more regularly. Running might appeal to your love of speed, but if you have dodgy knees, fast walking or

even swimming might be better for reducing injury risk. Use your Mindful Gauge to identify which activity you would like to explore.

Circle any of the activities that appeal to you:

Activities that you would like to consider (these may or may not be in the options above):

Do you need to prepare any equipment, look up the class timetable, coordinate with others, buy anything new to do the activity? Write your to-do list below:

SMALL STEPS AND ALTERNATIVES

There might be an activity that you would like to do but do not feel ready for right now. Applying the small-steps approach that we explored in Key 6, is there an activity that would be a step toward your preferred one?

Joan was mugged on her way home from work one evening. Prior to the attack she loved to hike in the hills near where she lived, but since the trauma she found leaving the house triggering. For the moment, working on ways to be calm at home was enough for her, but she missed the benefits she had previously gained from walking. She did not have enough money for a treadmill, but she found that simply walking on the spot while watching videos of mountain hikes was enjoyable. For now, it offered Joan the benefits of walking without having to leave the house, as well as the enjoyment of beautiful mountain views.

As Joan's recovery progressed, and she gradually gained confidence to leave the house, she began with short walks during daylight hours around her neighborhood. In addition, she often went with her dearest friend, which helped her to feel safe as well as companioned and thereby less isolated.

Ali loved yoga. They enjoyed the social aspect of being part of a group class and the teacher was warm and friendly. However, Ali found some of the yoga poses triggering. Whenever they were lying on their back, they felt the warning signs of a flashback. Ali decided to speak to their yoga teacher about helping them find alternative postures whenever the rest of the class was lying down. Ali was a little shy, worried about being the odd one out, and worried the class teacher would be insulted.

To their relief, Ali's yoga teacher was very understanding, and took some time before the next class to explore what felt right for Ali. Ali found that they could do almost exactly the same as the rest of the group, but sitting up instead of lying down. At the next class, Ali did their seated yoga exercises when the rest of the class lay down, and no one even noticed.

In some cases, your limitation might be financial. If you would like to join a gym but the membership is too great a cost at the moment, then you might consider trying similar workouts at home or in a park; there are many free workout videos on the internet. Local sports clubs are often a great way to try a sport without committing to buying all of the equipment yourself, and it can be a way to meet others who are new to the activity.

METHOD

1. Write the activity that you would like to do but for which you have a limitation around doing it exactly as it is.
2. Write the limitation in the circle.
3. In the circles around it, write a variety of alternative options, or ways that the activity could be adapted to your current ability or means. This could be doing the activity indoors, like Joan, or adapting the activity to leave out any parts you find triggering or overwhelming, like Ali. If you have trouble thinking of ideas, asking a friend or the coach/instructor of a similar activity may help you to identify alternative options.
4. Imagine trying out the alternative or adaptation. Use your Mindful Gauge to assess whether it needs further adaptation.

Notice whether you need any support to do the activity as is or adapted. Perhaps you need to speak to the class instructor or utilize a piece of equipment.

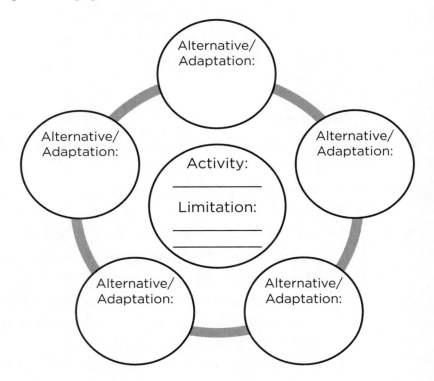

MOVEMENT IN NATURE

There is a plethora of research that shows being in nature is beneficial for mental well-being. Finding an activity that takes place outdoors may offer additional benefits to you.

Feeling connected to the natural world can bring a greater sense of belonging. Attuning to the changes that seasons and weather bring to birds, other animals, and plants might help you to remember and accept your own need to adapt, rest, and play.

If, as it was for Joan, leaving the house might be too much right now, consider alternatives such as looking at the tree outside your window or at an image or video of a landscape that appeals to you. In fact, there is research that shows that simply looking at images of nature aids recovery from stress. Research has also found that houseplants can have a positive effect on your mood.

Including contact with nature in your exercise plan could increase its value for you. Here are a few ideas:

- Many public parks have workout equipment that you can use for free.
- You could plot your walking route to include passing your favorite tree.
- Digging a community garden might be a great way to incorporate movement, nature, and social engagement.

METHOD

1. Would you like to include nature in the activity of your choice?
2. Read the suggestions below, adding any others you think of.
3. In the flower diagram below, write the ways you will include nature into your exercise activity.
4. Use your Mindful Gauge to assess whether including nature adds to your feeling of well-being.

Workout in the park.	Post nature photographs where you do your movement activity.	If indoors, look out the window while you exercise.
Listen to a birdsong or nature recording while doing your activity.	Plan a walking, cycling, or running route that includes a park or nature areas.	Watch nature videos while doing your activity.
Have a vase of flowers or houseplants nearby.	Do your activity in your garden or on your balcony.	Try a nature-based activity such as gardening.

In the petals, write the way(s) you plan to include nature with your movement activity.

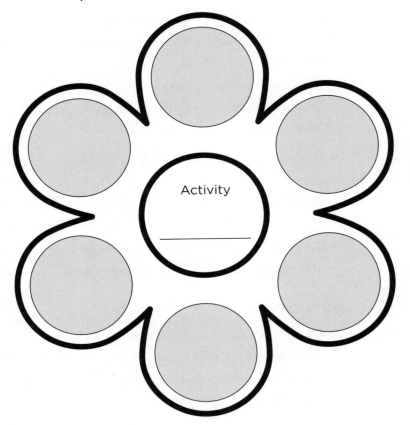

1. Arrange to try the activities you have chosen, one at a time.
2. If an activity is a team sport or a class, you may need to do some research to find the right team or class for you. Teachers are often very different, so if you try a class and it is not right for you then it would be worth trying a different teacher or two before dismissing the activity altogether.

Complete the table below to work out which activity would be a good match for you.

Activity			
Cost			
Equipment needed			
Accessibility (i.e., does it need to be done in a specific environment?)			
Alone/group/class/ team/friend			
Mindful Gauge response—imagining doing it			
Date, time, and place to try it			
Mindful Gauge response—while doing it			
Mindful Gauge response—afterward			

FIND AN EXERCISE BUDDY

Contact and support can be great resources for recovery. Exercising with a friend can also help you to keep going, as you are more likely to stick to a plan when the two of you are motivating and supporting each other.

Research has shown that exercising in synchrony with others can improve self-esteem and enhance mood. This could be a class, where everyone is following an instructor, or a workout video that you could follow at home.

Consider whether any of your friends and acquaintances are already exercising in activities you might like to try, or whether they have spoken about being keen to start. It might be that you are not ready to exercise with a friend at the moment, that the friend lives too far away, or that your schedules do not correspond. However, you can still offer and gain support through telephone and email.

METHOD

1. In the box below, make a list of people you know who exercise regularly or might be keen to start.
2. Write the activity that they do in the box, and include the days and times when they currently do it. Talk with them about how you can support each other. If it is by telephone, decide when you will call each other and the type of support you would each like.

Friend	Activity	Days/Times	How you can support each other (e.g., do the activity together/call and encourage each other)

SET UP RECORD KEEPING

In the early 1980s, when Babette was struggling with the worst of her own PTSD, her therapist suggested that building additional muscle tone through exercise might help her more easily stabilize, as well as contain the high arousal she was experiencing. She found that walking did help but was not enough. So, she decided to try specific strength training, but was daunted because she had never done anything like that before, and did not think she would like it. Additionally, she did not want to go to a gym. So, she did a little research (not online in those days) and settled on five exercises that would specifically build muscle in her legs and also in her arms. She knew that it would be hard for her to be conscientious about it, so she got some graph paper to log her progress, figuring a visual aid would help to keep her engaged. Across the top she used one square per day, noting the date. Along the side she listed the five exercises. Then, each day, she would write how many repetitions she did of each exercise. She was nervous about beginning so she started very small, just five reps of each exercise. Then each day she increased by one rep until she felt it was a good workout for her—not too little and not too much. The graph really helped her to stick with it, as she did not like to see blanks for days when she skipped the routine. Keeping the graph filled in became an additional motivating tool.

A log, graph, or chart may also be a useful tool for you to maintain a regular activity schedule. You may choose to add to your usual wall chart or calendar. An app that tracks progress might also be useful; many give incentives that boost progress, such as trophies when you reach specific goals. It may be easier to keep track of your progress using a chart specific to your activity.

To keep you motivated, you might mark your progress by giving yourself gold stars, or adding money to a jar each time you exercise and using that money for a special treat.

1. How will you take note of your activity progress?
    Chart/graph/add to diary/use table below/other: _____

2. How will you encourage your progress? Stickers/a treat once you have completed a number of sessions/money added to a treat jar each time you exercise/something else: _____

Day	Time	Activity	Description	Progress
Monday				
Tuesday				
Wednesday				
Thursday				
Friday				
Saturday				
Sunday				

HABIT-MAKING MOVEMENT

For those of you who have previously tried to quit a bad habit, you may have noticed that things tend to become habitual when linked with other activities. For example, someone who stops smoking often gets pangs of longing for a cigarette when drinking coffee or at a bar. Recently, while having coffee with a friend, she told me (author, Vanessa) about her longing for a cigarette: "I always had one with my afternoon latte."

Likewise, when looking to create a healthy habit, linking things together can be a great way to form the good habit. You may find it helps to set a regular time of day for your activity, for example, going out for a walk right after getting dressed in the morning, or going to a yoga class that takes place during your lunch break.

It is easy to get out of the routine of exercise when you are on vacation, sick, or even just tired. So, it might be good to make a plan for those and other possible situations where you might easily break the exercise habit you have worked so diligently to develop. What will help you get back into the swing of your routine when you have not exercised for a day or more?

Ali usually does some yoga practice at home after their morning shower. When they have other plans at that time and cannot do the full exercise, they still go to the spot where they would practice, roll out their mat, roll it back up, and carry on with their day. That way their habit is maintained. When they are ill, if they are awake and well enough, they take a moment at the time they would usually practice to remember standing in the spot where they practice and imagine rolling out the mat and rolling it back up again.

METHOD

1. Consider the time of day when you would prefer to do your activity.
2. Note down the daily routines you already have at that time of day.
3. Consider which daily routine would be best linked to your exercise activity so that right after you do that daily routine you then start your exercise activity. Use your Mindful Gauge to help you decide.

4. Circle the daily routine that you think would be best linked to your exercise activity.

5. Use your Mindful Gauge to assess whether that would work out or whether a different daily routine would be better.

Time of day:	Your current daily routines at that time:	The exercise activity to do afterward or alongside:
e.g., Morning	e.g., Get out of bed; brush teeth; shower; eat breakfast	e.g., Walk in the park

Make a note of ways you could make a symbolic gesture to mark the time for your exercise activity when you have other plans or are otherwise unable to do it. Ali went to the place where they did their activity, or imagined going there. They rolled out a yoga mat and then rolled it back up. What would be a similar marker for your chosen activity?

TIME-SAVING MOVEMENT HABITS

As we discussed in the previous exercise, linking activities together can strengthen habits. Many people find exercise a challenge to fit into their day. If this sounds like you, then you might consider taking mini–movement breaks throughout the day, rather than attempting to find a time slot big enough to fit in an entire movement session. Some people find that they simply prefer periods of mini-exercising, rather than setting aside time for a specific sport or activity. Below are some ideas on how to link mini–movement breaks, in case this sounds like something you would like to explore further. Our suggestions are not exhaustive, so you might come up with other combinations best suited to you.

Toni enjoyed the strength she felt from doing squats, but often found it difficult to make time in her day. She decided to do squats whenever she was waiting for the kettle to boil for her tea. Linking squats with boiling the kettle ensured that she had time available to do them, when she would otherwise have simply been standing still and waiting. The link between the kettle and the squats also served as a useful reminder to actually do them. Over time this became a consistent habit for her.

Freddy found it difficult to remember to do his strengthening exercises so he decided to link them with the commercial breaks in his favorite TV show. He kept his free weights by the television as an additional reminder.

We encourage you to start small and aim to create a habit that feels comfortable enough that you will want to continue. For example, Toni started by doing just one gentle squat each time she waited for the kettle; the next day she did two. After two weeks, she found that 10 was a good number for feeling the strength in her legs without getting too tired.

METHOD

1. Consider which of your daily activities or tasks you might be able to link a movement exercise to.
2. Test out whether it would actually work. Drinking coffee and dancing might not be a great partnership, but taking a walk while talking to your granddaughter on a cell phone might work well.

3. In the circles below, write a daily activity that you could link with an exercise activity.

4. Test it out. Use your Mindful Gauge to help work out whether this is a good match or whether there might be a better pairing.

5. Start with just one link, making it a small step that is something relatively easy for you to accomplish.

You may wish to write a reminder where the activity takes place while you are still getting into the habit. For example, Toni put a sticky note with the word "squats" next to her kettle. Freddy put his free weights next to the television, where he would see them. Below are some examples of everyday activities that could be linked to an exercise. Add your own ideas to the blank boxes.

Waiting for the kettle to boil	Waiting in line—for the bus, store, etc.	Watching TV	Reading emails
Speaking on the phone	Waiting for the toaster, oven, etc.	Reading	Brushing your teeth
Washing dishes	Commercial breaks	Listening to the radio/audiobooks	

Here are examples of exercises that could be linked to an everyday activity. Add your own ideas to the blank boxes.

Doing squats	Planking (on the floor or leaning against a wall)	Walking, jumping, or jogging on the spot	Lifting and lowering your heels
Lifting weights/arm curls	Balancing on one leg	Jumping rope	Muscle tensioning (see exercise in this Key)
Dancing	Walking outdoors	Doing jumping jacks	Exercise-biking

For example,

Whenever I wait for the kettle to boil, I stand on one leg.

Whenever I wait in line, I lift and lower my heels.

Whenever I speak to Maya, I walk on the spot.

Whenever I _____, I _____.

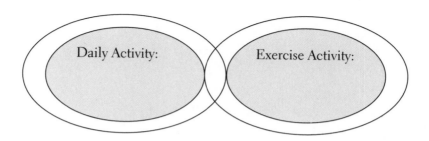

Daily Activity: Exercise Activity:

The next set of exercises contains suggestions of activities that are intended to help you feel strong, mindful, and present. Use your Mindful Gauge to help you assess the usefulness to you, and adapt the exercises to best suit your body and your needs. In Key 1 you will find exercises for mindful walking, which may also be useful to help you get moving.

POSTURE

Research suggests that posture and mood are linked. *Grey's Anatomy* demonstrated a good example of this in season 11, episode 14, when Amelia adopted a Superwoman pose to give her a feeling of competence before performing a particularly gnarly surgery. Though there is some dispute about the reliability of the research that this theory is based on, you can test its effectiveness for yourself.

While you are sitting reading this book, first slump and notice whether there is a change in your mood or energy level, or even in your ability to concentrate. Then sit up straight and check out the same. Is there any difference? You might try shifting your posture in a variety of situations throughout your day or week when you think of it. Finding what kind of posture is most beneficial for you in various situations could be useful. For example, when you want to relax, a good slump might be in order. However, if you want to ask your boss for a raise, it might be to your advantage to sit up straight. You might even notice a difference (for better or worse) in how others respond to you, depending on your posture. Consider, for instance, how teenagers often change their posture depending on who they are with. A teen walking around with a straight back might be frowned upon in their peer group but complimented by their parents. For fun you could play with your posture and see what happens inside you and with those you encounter.

Experimenting with and noticing whether your posture has an effect on your mood may give you an additional tool when exercising that can increase the benefits. In activities where you are standing, walking, or sitting, bring awareness to your posture and adjust it according to what helps you be most successful.

Luca spent lots of time walking. She sometimes felt a little anxious walking outdoors and so, to start with, she walked at home during commercial breaks in her favorite TV show. She noticed that she felt reluctant to do the walking she had committed to because she felt sluggish and tired, and that her shoulders ached a little afterward. Exploring her posture, Luca found that it mirrored her reluctance. Her shoulders were slumped and her head was dropped toward the floor. Experimenting, she found that if she walked with her shoulders back and her chest and chin lifted a little, she felt much more present and invested in the walking; it became easier to do. In addition, her shoulders ached less and she started to look forward to walking during the commercial breaks.

As we stress throughout this book: No matter the research, what is important is how any intervention, exercise, or task feels to you and works for you. Some people may feel a sense of power and a lightening of their mood when they expand their chest and open their arms, like Wonder Woman or Pavarotti, while others may find such positions too vulnerable or anxiety provoking. Experiment to find what works for you.

1. Hunch your shoulders forward, round your back, and let your head hang down.

How do you feel in this position? Consider your mood, thoughts, images, body sensations.

What would you think about someone else's mood if you saw them in this position?

2. Holding your head up, lift your chest away from your belly, draw your shoulder blades a little toward each other, lift your chin.

> How do you feel in this position? Consider your mood, thoughts, images, body sensations.
>
> What would you think about someone else's mood if you saw them in this position?

3. Move between the two postures described above, and find where your body is most comfortable and you are able to be most present.

> How do you feel in this position? Consider your mood, thoughts, images, body sensations.
>
> What would you think about someone else's mood if you saw them in this position?

CONNECTING WITH YOUR STRENGTH

Feeling and developing the strength of your body can help create a sense of power as well as containment. Adapting strength exercises to best suit your body is essential. Luckily, there are many different types of strengthening exercises that can be easily adapted to suit most people.

Sally had panic attacks whenever she was doing exercises on the floor. She was reminded of being in a similar position when she was attacked. She found that doing planks standing against the wall, instead of lying down, gave her a feeling of strength and control. Even if you do not get triggered as Sally did, aim for exercise positions that help you to feel strong and in charge.

It is important not to exert yourself to the point where you feel fatigued; otherwise, you risk losing that sense of power that you have cultivated. Some exercise instructors push their students to "do it till it burns" or even until they become nauseated. We could certainly argue whether that kind of extremism is good for anyone, but surely it cannot be good for someone who wants to feel more comfortable in their body and feel in control. Alternatively, we recommend that you continually assess how you are feeling and build up slowly, in small steps. It might be one movement or a few, or it might be holding a position, and so on. Some people feel most secure when feeling strength in their arms, others in their legs or other parts of their body; notice what is best for you. Also, finishing your exercise while you feel you could or want to do a bit more is a much better strategy than exercising to the point of dreading the next time.

Once you have practiced your strength exercises over a period of time it may become possible to connect with the feeling of strength simply by remembering or imagining doing that exercise. This can be useful in difficult situations where it would not be appropriate to do it physically, and can be practiced between physical exercise sessions. Remembering a resource, such as strength, in that way can also come in handy in a stressful situation where having a sense of your physical power would help you to feel emotionally stronger or help you to stand your ground in an argument. Below are some possibilities.

PLANK AGAINST A WALL

Place your hands on the wall and take a few steps back. Push with your hands, arms, and feet. Allow your spine to feel long. When you are ready to increase the exertion, you could try bending your elbows or your knees while leaning into the wall and then pushing back into the original position, like doing a push-up against the wall.

This can also be done in a chair. Bring the chair a little nearer than arms' distance from the wall. Make sure the chair is stable and does not move as you push away.

SQUATS

Stand with your feet shoulder-width apart and bend your knees, lowering down. Assess how much to lower to notice your leg muscles engage but without becoming too fatigued. You may prefer to stay in that position for a few seconds and then stand back up or to move in and out of the squat position. If you feel wobbly, stand in front of a wall or chair, and use your hands to steady yourself.

ON TIPTOE

Standing, or sitting, with your feet a little apart, slowly lift up and lower down your heels. If you feel wobbly it may be useful to keep one hand on a wall or chair to stabilize yourself. You may find that the slower you lower and lift, the greater the feeling of strength.

Below are some additional suggestions of ways to connect with the strength of your body. Add more that you remember bringing you that feeling of strength. Try some out and assess which are useful for you. Circle the ones that are beneficial.

Push ups	Squeezing hand into a fist	Pull ups	Climbing stairs
Walking through water, at a pool		Lifting weights	Rowing machine

MUSCLE TONING

You may have been told by one or more people—friend, family member, professional—that you should relax more. If that helps, terrific. However, if it does not, you may have felt as if there is something wrong with you that you feel more anxious or agitated when you try to relax. Here is some good news: If that sounds like you, you are not alone. There are actually a good many people—not only those with trauma histories—who actually become more anxious or distressed in other ways from trying to relax or engage in activities that are geared for that purpose, such as yoga, massage, meditation, and so on. There is even a name for the phenomenon: *relaxation-induced anxiety.* If this sounds like you, then read below, as we have a very useful, if unexpected, alternative to suggest.

Increasing your muscle tone, that is, becoming *more* tense, may be a better way for you to be more calm than any kind of "relaxation" activity. In fact, if you set your goal to be more calm rather than to be more relaxed, you might have a more satisfying result.

In addition, adding tone to your muscles can be a powerful way to develop a sense of physical as well as emotional containment. When emotions feel as though they might spill outside of you, developing a sturdy outer shell can give you a sense of solidity. Think of a plastic bottle of carbonated soda. You might remember from opening those kinds of bottles that the contents are under a lot of pressure. When you screw off the cap, there is often a "psst" sound as the gas releases, or even an overflow of the contents if the bottle has been dropped or shaken up. The firmness of the outer surface of that bottle is what makes it possible to contain all of that pressure. Imagine what would happen if the contents were in a flimsy plastic bag instead. Likely the beverage would spill all over the place; the flimsy bag could not contain it. In a similar way, your outer surface, of which your muscles are a part, need to be strong enough to help you to contain your emotions and the activation energy that may be there from your traumatic stress. The firmer your muscles are, the better they will be able to help you to feel contained and in control.

Tensing in different muscles and muscle groups may elicit different responses. Adding tension to your arms may feel different than tensing the sides of your legs. There may be a difference from right to left. We encourage you to experiment while using your Mindful Gauge to help you assess your response to increasing muscle tone and its usefulness for you.

Rather than tensing and then releasing straightaway, as some other practices do, the way to increase tone for greater calm and control is to release slowly. That will help to foster the feeling of containment. First, just hold the tension until your muscle barely begins to be tired, then release the tension gradually in small increments, over 10–15 seconds. The aim is to retain a small amount of the tension even at the end. That will help to build muscle tone and your ability to contain and control your stress and emotions.

(Caveat: If, while tensing a muscle, or after you release it, you feel spacey, anxious, or nauseated, stop and take that one off your list, at least for a while. You may be able to try it again after you have further recovered from your trauma. Which muscles help and which do not can change over time.)

You can use these same instructions with any muscle or muscle group. Below are a few to get you started[*]:

1. **Sides of Legs:** Stand with your feet a little less than shoulder-width apart, knees neither locked nor bent. Press your knees out directly to the side so that you can feel tension up the sides of your legs from knee to hip.

2. **Left Arm:** Sit or stand with arms crossed right over left, your right hand covering your left elbow. First, your right hand provides resistance as your left arm lifts directly away from your body. You may feel tension in the forward-directed part of your upper arm from shoulder to elbow. Next, your right hand provides resistance to the back of your elbow as your left arm pushes directly left. You may

---

[*] Exercises as taught to Babette at the Bodynamic Institute in Copenhagen, Denmark, in their training program 1988–1992. See Babette Rothschild, *The Body Remembers* (2000).

feel tension in the left-directed part of the upper arm from shoulder to elbow.

3. **Right Arm**: Sit or stand with your arms crossed left over right. Your left hand should be covering the right elbow. First, your left hand provides resistance as your right arm lifts directly away from your body. You may feel tension in the forward-directed part of your upper arm from shoulder to elbow. Next, your left hand provides resistance to the back of your elbow as your right arm pushes directly right. You may feel tension in the right-directed part of your upper arm from shoulder to elbow.

4. **Thighs:** Sitting in a chair, place both feet flat on the floor. Press weight onto your feet just until you feel tension build in your thighs. Make sure not to press so hard that you tip your chair over backward.

MOVING WITH BALANCE

An exercise in Key 3 explored balancing objects to notice whether it was a useful tool for focus and presence. In this exercise we apply the small-steps approach of Key 6 to balancing, and add in the potential benefits of movement of this Key.

Research shows a connection between PTSD and anxiety, on the one hand, and difficulties with balance and vestibular issues, on the other. This can add to a general feeling of instability. Improving balance can bring a sense of mastery and stabilization, as well as greater presence and focus.

Though stress can be a negative experience, a little stress enables us to be active, alert, and ready to act. That is why, for instance, someone might have a cup of tea or coffee to help them meet a deadline. The caffeine raises the body's stress level slightly and gives some extra oomph for following through. This active alert stress may be present in many of the movement exercises. You might notice an increase in heart rate, cool hands and feet, a quickening of your breath, and perspiration. Though this is not a cardiovascular or aerobic exercise, the level of focus may activate an active and alert response. It can be useful to use your Mindful Gauge to assess the level of challenge for you, noticing when the active and alert response moves from being helpful into bringing a feeling of discomfort. Reduce the challenge if you notice signs of overwhelm.

FIND YOUR CENTER

You can do this standing or sitting. Try to keep your spine lengthened, and you may wish to place a hand on a wall or the back of a chair for greater stability. If standing, you may find greater stability with your feet set shoulder-width apart.

1. Slowly take your weight forward, judging how far you can go without any risk of falling. If you are standing, take most of your weight into your toes. If you are sitting, take it into the front of your seat

bones. The first time you do it you may wish to be more cautious, as you work this out.

2. Next, bring your weight backward, judging how far back you can go without risking that you will fall. The first time you do it you may wish to be more cautious, as you work this out. If you are standing, take the majority of your weight onto your heels. If you are sitting take it onto the back of your seat bones.

3. Next, slowly rock forward and backward, reducing the distance between each until you find a central point: not too far forward, not too far backward, but, as with Goldilocks, just right.

4. Once you are centered forward and backward, explore side to side in the same way.

5. Lean over to the right side as far as feels okay, then slowly lean over to the left.

6. Move between these two places, reducing the movement each time until you find the center: not too far left, not too far right, but just right in the middle.

7. Play with small adjustments forward and back and left and right until you find where your body feels centered. You will recognize your center spot when you are needing the least effort to hold yourself upright.

BUILDING-BLOCKS BALANCE TO INCREASE BODY BALANCE AND MINDFUL FOCUS

1. As in the exercise in Key 3, balance two objects, such as building blocks, holding on to the one on the bottom. Another possibility would be to balance one object, such as a pen or pencil on your finger, or a tennis ball on the back of your hand.

2. This might be challenge enough. If the object drops, start again.

3. However, if you want to add more challenge, some suggestions are below. Try only one additional challenge at a time (in any order) and use your Mindful Gauge to assess which are useful to you to increase your ability to focus.

Next steps might include:

Walk while balancing the blocks	Sit down and stand back up	Turn a circle
Lift the blocks above your head and back down	Swap hands	Add a third block on top

We also encourage you to experiment and think up your own next steps to suit you.

BOOK AND BALL BALANCE

These exercises get increasingly challenging. Use the small-steps approach from Key 6: Start with the first, then if you feel you would like more challenge to stay focused and present, try the second, and so on. Move to a different step only if you notice that the challenge is not enough to keep you focused and present. Remember, the goal is to be focused and present rather than a great balancer!

1. Balance a ball on a book.
2. Walk around, keeping the ball balanced on the book.
3. Try walking at different speeds.
4. Experiment walking sideways and backward.
5. Bounce the ball on the book and catch it with the book.
6. Balance the ball on the book and walk around, sit down, stand back up.
7. Explore all the ways you can move and balance the ball.

Key Review

Did you remember to use your Mindful Gauge to evaluate the exercises in this chapter? If not, was that by choice or because you forgot?

	Did this exercise help, or make you feel worse?	If it helped, what reaction did you have that told you it helped? (For example, felt calmer or stronger or more present.)
Find Your Activity		
Small Steps and Alternatives		
Movement in Nature		
Try Them Out		
Find an Exercise Buddy		
Set Up Record Keeping		

If you forgot, consider whether you want to go back and do that. Once you have completed an exercise you may wish to jot down your response and its effectiveness for you in the table.

If it helped, could it be adapted to help more? How?	If it helped, when do you plan to use it?	If it did not help, could you change or adapt it to better suit you? How?

	Did this exercise help, or make you feel worse?	If it helped, what reaction did you have that told you it helped? (For example, felt calmer or stronger or more present.)
Habit-Making Movement		
Time-Saving Movement Habits		
Posture		
Connecting With Your Strength		
Muscle Toning		
Moving With Balance		

If it helped, could it be adapted to help more? How?	If it helped, when do you plan to use it?	If it did not help, could you change or adapt it to better suit you? How?

KEY 8 MAKE LEMONADE

> How wonderful it is that nobody need wait a single
> moment before starting to improve the world.
>
> —ANNE FRANK, *Anne Frank's Tales from the Secret Annex:*
> *A Collection of Her Short Stories, Fables*
> *and Lesser-Known Writings*

> Those who are happiest are those who do the most
> for others.
>
> —BOOKER T. WASHINGTON, *Up from Slavery*

One of Vanessa's favorite things to spot when out walking is the phenomenon of nature overcoming adversity and thriving. She loves to see flowers growing out of concrete, foliage out of derelict buildings, and the deformities of trees that have been damaged but found a new way or shape in which to grow and bear fruit. These observations fill Vanessa with a sense of hope and remind her that no matter how devastating the challenges humans face, anyone can recover, and can find or create ways to make their lives useful and fulfilling.

The name of this Key is taken from the commonly known saying coined by Elbert Hubbard in 1915. He wrote an obituary for an actor, praising his achievements in spite of his disabilities: "He picked up the lemons that Fate had sent him and started a lemonade stand."

This Key explores this idea of making something good despite the adversity you may have experienced. This does not mean that we take those experiences lightly, or wish to diminish the difficulties you have faced. Both authors of this book have themselves experienced trauma and suffered from the debilitating symptoms of PTSD. We have been in your shoes, so to speak. And one of the ways we have each made lemonade is writing this book in the hopes of helping you and others.

There has been varied research into the benefits of helping others. Those being helped benefit, of course, but the research also shows incredible rewards for the helpers themselves. Studies show that helping others can improve physical health, including lowering blood pressure (Sneed & Cohen, 2013), improving cardiovascular health (Schreier et al., 2013), decreasing cholesterol, reducing physical pain (Wang et al., 2019), and increasing lifespan (Okun et al., 2013). Research also shows improved mental health, including a reduction in stress and depression. When we help others, the brain releases the "feel good" chemicals serotonin, dopamine, and oxytocin, causing a lift in mood.

Of course, in the immediate aftermath of a traumatic experience, it may not be possible to make lemonade. However, as time passes, it may be something that you could benefit from doing. Considering what you might like to do to help others when you are recovered enough could offer something to look forward to, and bring a sense of determination and purpose.

Research has shown that gaining a sense of purpose and meaning can be hugely beneficial in recovery from trauma. Helping others can also provide you with something to focus on in addition to recovering from trauma, which can often feel all-consuming. Making space for other things in your life can add to a sense of having control, which, as we have discussed, can be invaluable to trauma recovery.

Where whole communities have been affected by trauma, such as with natural or human caused disasters, acting immediately to help others might be possible and beneficial. It can bring a sense of togetherness and diminish feelings of isolation. In the recent COVID-19 pandemic the whole world was affected, yet throughout the countries of the world people helped each other (and continue to help) with acts of generosity and kindness every single day.

During COVID-19, many people used their individual skills to help in whatever ways they could: grocery shopping for sick or high-risk neighbors they had barely spoken to before; dusting off sewing machines to make extra masks for friends who were nurses or doctors; donating items to food banks; waving or smiling through the window at passersby; and waving while walking past windows of shut-ins. Despite the realities of tragedy, fear, and isolation, those who offered even tiny acts of kindness reported gaining a sense of belonging, hope, and meaning.

It is common for individuals and groups who have experienced adversity to be spurred into action to help others so that they are less likely to experience similar trauma, or to make their own recovery safer and easier. In that way, many in the helping professions, including therapists and counselors, often choose such work because they have experienced trauma themselves. For the most part, trauma professionals (including the authors of this book) are wounded healers hoping to make lemonade in the form of helping their traumatized clients and even, sometimes, preventing PTSD.

Trauma can lead to feelings of isolation and loneliness, particularly if the traumatized person does not know others who have been likewise affected. Getting involved in easing the lives of those in need can help to counteract a feeling of isolation, as well as offering a sense of overcoming circumstances and effecting change.

A variety of charities and organizations were set up by people that were impacted by trauma themselves. They include Mothers Against Drunk Driving, set up by a grieving mother who wanted to reduce alcohol-related road accidents; and the Suzy Lamplugh Trust, set up by Suzy's parents after her disappearance, with the aim of decreasing the risk of violence and aggression in communities.

Making lemonade can, but does not need to, involve creating or participating in that kind of big project. It can absolutely be much simpler: helping a neighbor with their shopping, walking a dog at a shelter, or babysitting to give a lone parent some respite. Like everything else, to be successful for you, making lemonade must be individually tailored and timed to your needs and tastes. Make sure to not attempt tasks you would hate or be triggered by, or something that is scheduled at a time that is inconvenient to you.

In addition, take care with choosing whom you aim your help toward. If a person or group rejects your offer of help, try not to take it personally; there may be a variety of reasons that have nothing to do with you. Instead, move on and ask someone else.

Working out what kind of help you want to offer is important. Make sure that whatever you choose does not increase the symptoms of your trauma. Working toward preventing a similar trauma from happening again might be a long-term goal, such as supporting abused children, but notice whether an idea triggers worse symptoms. As we explored in Key 6, we encourage you to take small steps; do not attempt too much too soon.

The exercises in this chapter will help you to determine whether making lemonade is useful for you at the moment, what might be a good activity for you right now, what you might like to do in the future, and how to help others while looking after your own needs and facilitating your own recovery.

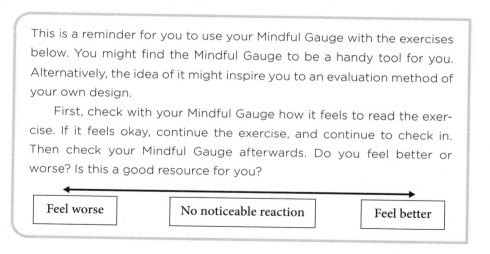

This is a reminder for you to use your Mindful Gauge with the exercises below. You might find the Mindful Gauge to be a handy tool for you. Alternatively, the idea of it might inspire you to an evaluation method of your own design.

First, check with your Mindful Gauge how it feels to read the exercise. If it feels okay, continue the exercise, and continue to check in. Then check your Mindful Gauge afterwards. Do you feel better or worse? Is this a good resource for you?

| Feel worse | No noticeable reaction | Feel better |

WHAT DO I VALUE NOW?

Following a traumatic experience, it may seem as though how you think about things, particularly your values or beliefs, has shifted. Some things about you will definitely stay the same, while others may change. Considering this for herself, nature enthusiast and coauthor, Vanessa, was reminded of a National Geographic Documentary that follows the reintroduction of gray wolves into Yellowstone National Park after being extinct in the area for one hundred years. The documentary describes the multitude of changes following the wolves' return.* Elk populations reduced, increasing vegetation, which had a knock-on effect throughout the area, including greater tree root structures, less erosion, increased numbers of beavers, fish, otters, and songbirds, to name a few. Despite the many changes, much of the fundamentals of the park stayed the same. It still had water, weather, trees, animals, birds, and so on. The rangers then faced the challenge of adjusting how they made decisions about the park. They could no longer make decisions based on how it was before the reintroduction of the wolves, as many of those decisions were no longer relevant or appropriate. It became imperative to first acknowledge the changes, the altered landscape, and adapt their choices to the new environment.

The same idea applies to you: As you recover from your traumatic experience or experiences, your inner landscape, and even perhaps your environmental landscape, is changing. Taking stock of what is important to you *now* can help with large and small decision-making, as well as giving you a more solid sense of self and your current situation. You may find that the fundamentals of what is important to you are the same, or you might notice changes in your values since your experience of trauma.

Following the exercise below, Ffion realized that stability had become one of her most important values. Being able to predict her day, live in the same house, know her route to work, and see the same faces each day brought her a greater sense of calm and happiness. Prior to her traumatic experience, she did not feel that stability was important at all, preferring to be spontaneous and unpredictable. That was a big shift for

---

* https://www.nationalgeographic.org/media/wolves-yellowstone/

her and took some getting used to. Ffion also noticed that other values remained the same, for example, she continued to value success and leadership. She decided to do this values exercise each year and put a reminder in her calendar, so that she could keep track of changes and adjust her plans, decisions, and routine accordingly. Hers is a good idea; as our values and beliefs do not only change from trauma. They continue to shift as we get older, have various life experiences, meet new people, and so on.

Harvey noticed that he was not currently making decisions that prioritized the values he had listed as most important. The exercise revealed that he valued family and friendship over independence. However, he often leaned towards spending time alone or at work. Not only was he not spending his days as he truly wished to, but he was also missing out on resources that would benefit him. With the knowledge he gained from the exercise, he changed some of his habits. For example, having lunch with his brother instead of at his desk, and running with a friend more often instead of running alone. He found that adapting his usual activities to meet his actual values gave him a greater sense of calm and satisfaction.

METHOD

1. Read the different values in each of the boxes and circle 1–10 on the scale of importance that value would be for you now. Use your Mindful Gauge to help.

    There might be values not listed here that are important to you. Add them in the empty boxes. Make sure to define the values according to what they mean to you. For example, "beauty" might be looking your best, or it could mean spending time in beautiful places, or even surrounding yourself with things you find attractive.

    For example:

Control		
Not important		Very important
1 2 3 4 5 6 7 **(8)** 9 10		

Beauty		
Not important		Very important
1 2 **(3)** 4 5 6 7 8 9 10		

2. In the table that follows the terms, add those that you marked highest: the terms that were most important to you.

3. You might notice that you can group some of the values by choosing an appropriate term that covers several values. See if it is possible to reduce the list to ten most important values.

4. Order the values 1–10 according to their importance to you.

5. Read them through and use your Mindful Gauge to check that they are in the correct order and whether they represent your values now.

6. You might want to add the list to your journal, a note at your computer, or wherever you tend to record decisions. Notice whether knowing your values will help with decisions you want to make, or whether they highlight a resource that is important to you that you can bring more of into your life.

Note: There are no correct answers! No value is innately more important than another; only what is right for you.

Independence	
Not important	Very important
1 2 3 4 5 6 7 8 9 10	

Leadership	
Not important	Very important
1 2 3 4 5 6 7 8 9 10	

Kindness	
Not important	Very important
1 2 3 4 5 6 7 8 9 10	

Beauty	
Not important	Very important
1 2 3 4 5 6 7 8 9 10	

Control	
Not important	Very important
1 2 3 4 5 6 7 8 9 10	

Enjoyment	
Not important	Very important
1 2 3 4 5 6 7 8 9 10	

Tradition	
Not important	Very important
1 2 3 4 5 6 7 8 9 10	

Friendship	
Not important	Very important
1 2 3 4 5 6 7 8 9 10	

Family	
Not important	Very important
1 2 3 4 5 6 7 8 9 10	

Wealth	
Not important	Very important
1 2 3 4 5 6 7 8 9 10	

Order

Not important   Very important

1   2   3   4   5   6   7   8   9   10

Adventurousness

Not important   Very important

1   2   3   4   5   6   7   8   9   10

Routine

Not important   Very important

1   2   3   4   5   6   7   8   9   10

Modesty

Not important   Very important

1   2   3   4   5   6   7   8   9   10

Challenge

Not important   Very important

1   2   3   4   5   6   7   8   9   10

Community

Not important   Very important

1   2   3   4   5   6   7   8   9   10

Self-control

Not important   Very important

1   2   3   4   5   6   7   8   9   10

Reliability

Not important   Very important

1   2   3   4   5   6   7   8   9   10

Structure

Not important   Very important

1   2   3   4   5   6   7   8   9   10

Service

Not important   Very important

1   2   3   4   5   6   7   8   9   10

Tolerance

Not important   Very important

1   2   3   4   5   6   7   8   9   10

Excitement

Not important   Very important

1   2   3   4   5   6   7   8   9   10

Discretion

Not important   Very important

1   2   3   4   5   6   7   8   9   10

Hard work

Not important   Very important

1   2   3   4   5   6   7   8   9   10

Stability

Not important   Very important

1   2   3   4   5   6   7   8   9   10

Spontaneity

Not important   Very important

1   2   3   4   5   6   7   8   9   10

Intelligence

Not important   Very important

1   2   3   4   5   6   7   8   9   10

Fairness

Not important   Very important

1   2   3   4   5   6   7   8   9   10

Honesty

Not important   Very important

1 2 3 4 5 6 7 8 9 10

Reputation

Not important   Very important

1 2 3 4 5 6 7 8 9 10

Generosity

Not important   Very important

1 2 3 4 5 6 7 8 9 10

Loyalty

Not important   Very important

1 2 3 4 5 6 7 8 9 10

Faith/Religion/Spirituality

Not important   Very important

1 2 3 4 5 6 7 8 9 10

Intimacy

Not important   Very important

1 2 3 4 5 6 7 8 9 10

Teamwork/Cooperation

Not important   Very important

1 2 3 4 5 6 7 8 9 10

Status

Not important   Very important

1 2 3 4 5 6 7 8 9 10

Patriotism

Not important   Very important

1 2 3 4 5 6 7 8 9 10

Creativity

Not important   Very important

1 2 3 4 5 6 7 8 9 10

Health

Not important   Very important

1 2 3 4 5 6 7 8 9 10

Success

Not important   Very important

1 2 3 4 5 6 7 8 9 10

Advocacy

Not important   Very important

1 2 3 4 5 6 7 8 9 10

Equality

Not important   Very important

1 2 3 4 5 6 7 8 9 10

_____

Not important   Very important

1 2 3 4 5 6 7 8 9 10

_____

Not important   Very important

1 2 3 4 5 6 7 8 9 10

_____

Not important   Very important

1 2 3 4 5 6 7 8 9 10

_____

Not important   Very important

1 2 3 4 5 6 7 8 9 10

Add the values that you marked highest, that were most important to you, here. Depending on your personal scores, these might be the values that scored 9 or 10 or those above 5:

Value	Importance score
e.g., Advocacy	10
e.g., Status	7

You might notice that you can group some of the values by choosing an appropriate term that covers several values. See if it is possible to reduce the list to ten most important values.

e.g., Ffion decided to group "routine, stability, and order" since, to her, these meant the same thing.

Following this exercise, Ffion noticed how her values were currently reflected in her day-to-day life, she noted her regular attendance at board meetings and continuous professional development seminars as ways she expressed the importance she placed on success and hard work. Harvey recognized that his weekly visits to see his mom and regular calls to his sister represented his regard for family. Consider, and list below, how the values you have listed as most important to you are currently represented in your life at the moment.

Value	How it is represented in your life at the moment
e.g., Career Success	Regular attendance at board meetings and continuous professional development seminar

Next, notice where there are any gaps or where you would like to introduce more of a value into your life. Harvey identified he did not currently have many close friends who shared his interests. He decided that he would join a martial arts class and an evening pottery class, where he hoped to meet some new people. Ffion decided to spend more holidays at home, rather than going overseas, visiting her favorite people and places in her own neighborhood.

Write in the table any gaps you have noticed and ways you could introduce more of the value into your life.

Value	How you could increase this in your life
e.g., Friendship	*Join a martial arts class and an evening pottery class to meet new people.*

PAY IT FORWARD

Now that you have a clearer sense of the values that are most important to you, you may have an idea of the area you would want to focus your efforts to make lemonade. For example, safety and predictability were important values for Ffion. She decided to volunteer in her local community, she felt safer in the place she knew best. Volunteering locally also provided her with a greater network close to home that increased her feelings of safety in her neighborhood.

Take a moment to consider the people, animals, even nature, that have helped you in your recovery or at other times in your life. These might include your therapist, a supportive friend, the author of a book that brought you comfort, an artist whose painting lifted your spirits. It could also be your dog who encourages you to go out for a walk each day and cuddles with you when you are upset, or the bird that sings a joyful tune outside your bedroom window, helping you to wake up or cheering your mood.

In this exercise we make space to notice those who have helped in your recovery. It may be that you can pay it back, for example, putting a bird feeder out for that joyful bird in the winter. However, it may be that paying it back is not possible, and paying it forward is more appropriate. For example, that smile from a stranger that lifted your spirits may not be given back to the same stranger just when they need it, but you can pay it forward to another stranger who seems as though they would benefit from a friendly face.

The way you pay it forward does not have to be the same way that you received help. Considering what change you would like to see in the world might give you inspiration for a small step that you can make toward that change. Certainly, one of the easiest and most available ways to pay it forward is with simple acts of kindness: opening a door for someone, picking up a dropped object, carrying groceries up a flight of stairs, and so on.

1. Make a note of the help or support that you have received, no matter how small it seems. We encourage you to keep adding to this list

as you remember something or as you experience new forms of support. Remember to include human, animal, and nature support.

Who/what helped	What did they do?	How did you feel?

2. List the ways you could pay it back, such as putting out a feeder for the bird that sings, or helping the neighbor who shared their baking. It does not have to be paid back in the same way or at the same rate or value in which it was received. If you are unable to pay it back, use the next step to pay it forward.

WHO Who or what helped you	HOW The ways you could pay it back	WHEN Plan a date to do it

3. Consider how you might pay it forward. We have offered some options below. Use your Mindful Gauge to circle the ones that feel like things you could do. Make a note if you think of a specific person that would benefit or if you plan to keep it in mind when the opportunity arises with a stranger or someone you know. Add any more that you can think of.

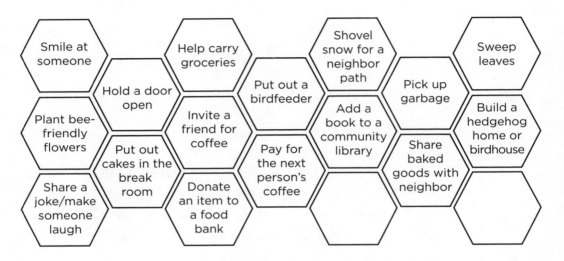

There may be a variety of ways that you can help others. You may choose to sign on as a volunteer for an organization or at a hospital or school. You may decide to ask a particular friend or neighbor if they need any help. You could also decide that you want to identify your skills and then be prepared to offer help spontaneously when the need arises, for example, offering to help a friend move to a new house, helping a child with their homework, or walking a dog for someone who is unable.

Babette shares what she has learned during her recovery using her skills for teaching and writing. Spurred on by both positive and negative experiences during her own recovery from PTSD, she helps people in a professional capacity by teaching other professionals and writing books and articles about safe and varied strategies for trauma recovery. Where possible, she also likes to help her nieces, nephews, and others to succeed in their studies and professional endeavors as she was supported and helped to succeed in her own. During the COVID-19 lockdown, she and her neighbors formed a supportive community of sorts via phone and text, helping one another with bigger and smaller tasks, or just keeping tabs on one another to make sure no one became isolated.

Vanessa used her skills and passions to make lemonade in various ways. Riding her bike had been a great resource in her recovery, helping her gain a feeling of strength and joy. Fixing bikes helped her focus and be grounded in the present moment. To pay that forward, she developed a community bike project, teaching people of all backgrounds how to ride, build, and fix bicycles. She started this project small during the time when she was still managing her PTSD symptoms. Her first steps involved giving advice via an online forum and fixing friends' broken bicycles at home. She found that even the smallest project task provided a needed counterpoint to her trauma recovery, and gave her a sense of purpose that came from helping others, including feelings of strength and belonging.

As Vanessa gained more control of her symptoms, she began taking small groups of women on bike rides in the community, then ran classes for asylum seekers and refugees. She also started ad hoc bike-mechanic classes in youth and community centers around her city. Eventually she found an affordable venue for the bike project and ended up winning an award for her contribution to the community. In this case Vanessa's small steps for paying it forward eventually led to something very big; however, that definitely does not have to be the case. Vanessa did not aim for such a major outcome; she just took lots of small steps in the same direction. The point is to take small steps, whether in the same direction or in many different directions. Helping a neighbor with their shopping one day, and then picking up litter another day, is just as beneficial, and can be just as rewarding as (and actually less stressful than) being the director of a charity.

Using a skill or interest you already have might offer you a way to help where you already have some confidence and motivation. That is how Vanessa ended up with her bike project, because she liked all those activities: riding, repairing, and assembling bikes. The point is to choose one or more activities that you enjoy and, step-by-step, build on that. However, if you have a skill or experience in something you are not interested in doing, then it is good to be aware of that too. Give yourself permission to say no as well as yes. It is important to connect with your inner Goldilocks from Key 1 and not do something that is not right for you.

METHOD

1. Consider the suggestions in the table below, using your Mindful Gauge to notice what seems like something you would like to do.
2. Circle any that you feel you have skills, passion, or interest in. Add any that are not listed. You do not need to pursue all of them, but gaining awareness of your varied interests and skills might be useful. You may be able to combine some into one activity.
3. In the gray boxes below the choices you have circled, write possibilities of what you would like to do with that skill. We have offered some suggestions to give you ideas.

In addition to the type of activity you would like to do, consider where and with whom you would prefer to do it.

Baking	Fixing and repairing	Sewing	Knitting
Bake for friends, soup kitchens, etc.	*Help neighbors, friends, or charities*	*Mend clothes, make nurses' face masks*	*Knit clothing for charities or friends*
Gardening	Cooking	Teaching/instructing	Woodwork
Help neighbors, school gardening clubs, community gardens	*Make food for a sick friend or neighbor, or help at a soup kitchen*	*Tutor a child or student you know*	*Teach a community class, make items for friends and neighbors*
Reading aloud	Listening, chatting/befriending	Dog walking	Child minding
Read aloud at local library, school, or nursing home	*Visit or call friends or people in hospital or care home*	*Walk dogs at animal shelters or for friends that need help*	*Offer respite to a parent you know*

Home improvement	Painting/decorating	Making things/craft	Drawing/painting/artwork
Help neighbors, friends, local charities, community and senior centers with odd jobs such as putting up shelves, building flat-pack furniture	*Help friends, neighbors, local charities, community and senior centers with painting and decorating jobs*	*Send out spontaneous useful gifts to friends*	*Share skills at a charity or school; paint a mural*
Cleaning	Medical skills	Driving	Physical strength
Help injured or disabled friends, or volunteer at charities	*Support a local sporting event or medical-aid charity*	*Collect groceries, help move to new house, visit hospital*	*Help people move to new house, carry shopping*
Animal care	Sports	Music	Translating
Pet-sit when people are away, volunteer at a shelter	*Coach or help out with a local team*	*Teach at a school or youth program*	*Assist at refugee charities*
Photographer/ videographer	_____	_____	_____

Document sporting and charity events, teach skills			

Animals	People	Nature	At home	Charity	Community	Outdoors

KINTSUGI

Kintsugi originates from the Japanese philosophy *wabi sabi*, which celebrates the beauty of imperfection and impermanence. Rather than throwing away broken pots, bowls, vases, and other objects, in the practice of *kintsugi* they are repaired to be as strong and useful as ever. But the practice does not end there. Following a repair, the visible cracks are painted with additional adhesive that contains real gold. The purpose is to highlight the break and the repair, rather than hiding it, and to make the object even more beautiful than before it was broken. You can find many examples via an online search of the term "kintsugi." You may be astounded at how beautiful a repaired bowl, which otherwise you would likely have thrown away, can be.

The parallel between the art of *kintsugi* and that of trauma recovery is an important one. What you have learned, the new knowledge you have gained in your own recovery from trauma, is precious. Though you may always have scars from your experiences, those scars can be transformed into something useful and beautiful with a little creativity and persistence.

Affi had been seriously injured and her best friend killed as the result of a cycling accident. She had physically recovered but developed symptoms of PTSD, including flashbacks and a feeling of panic.

Before Affi had completely recovered, she identified a variety of skills that she had developed following the trauma, including a range of resources and strategies that helped to manage her flashbacks and panic attacks. Much to her surprise, she found that she could put those skills to work helping her young niece, who was experiencing panic attacks at school whenever she had to speak in front of her class. Even though Affi was not comfortable with leaving her house, she was glad to meet up online. They arranged a time to talk about some of the skills Affi had learned for coping with panic attacks. She helped her niece to get in control of her anxiety and stay calm when she felt panic rising. The next week her niece called, excited to tell Affi that she had volunteered for show-and-tell and, for the first time, had been able to stay calm while in front of the class. She was very grateful. Affi felt incredibly proud that she had been able to share her knowledge and skills. In addition, she was very happy to be developing a deeper connection with her niece. As a result, she felt satisfaction in being able to help and, as a bonus, less alone.

In her training programs Babette often shows a video clip of a 6-year-old boy helping his 4-year-old brother calm down and avoid an impending temper tantrum by simply directing him to take a few deep breaths. Inspiringly, the little brother instantly calms down and the tantrum is averted. It is not clear from the short video how the older brother became so skilled and wise, but one can imagine it is something he learned in school. As demonstrated by these brothers, sharing the skills you have learned does not need to be formal or planned. It could be a spontaneous intervention to help yourself, someone you know, or even a stranger. It could be a good idea to take note of the skills you have gained and how you might use them so that they come to mind if the occasion arises. It might also raise your own sense of competency to write down and realize the skills that you have gained along the way in your life both before and following trauma.

When you are considering sharing the knowledge or skill you have, it is important that you do *not* feel the need to share *why* you gained that skill. It is not necessary, or even a good idea, to tell your trauma story when you are endeavoring to help someone else. In fact, it may be destabilizing for you, possibly both of you, to do so.

Search online for one or more videos on the art of *kintsugi*. And then consider whether you would like to repair something that is broken, or enhance in some way something you have repaired before. It can be anything: a cup, plate, bathroom tile, vase, flower pot, crack in your front porch or patio surface, and so on. It does not matter what it is. Repair it with the intention to further use it and with an eye to making the repair itself enhance the look, use, or value of the object. The point is to remember that something broken can be repaired and continue to be useful and, often, can be even more beautiful. You could also imagine how you would have repaired something now gone if you still had it.

1. Write or sketch a plan in the box on the folloiwing page for how you will repair it (or write or draw how you would repair the object if you still had it). If you still have the broken object, make a date to take some time to repair it.

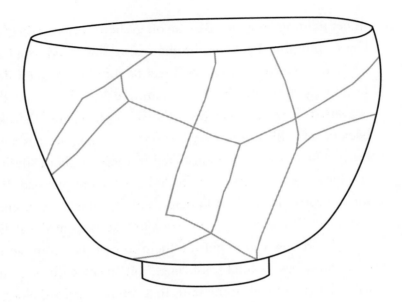

2. Write the skills and knowledge that you have gained in your recovery on the lines in the image below.

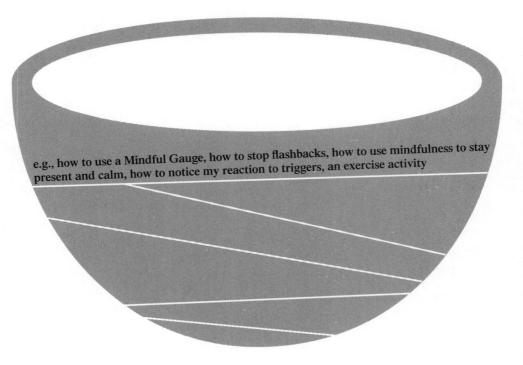

e.g., how to use a Mindful Gauge, how to stop flashbacks, how to use mindfulness to stay present and calm, how to notice my reaction to triggers, an exercise activity

3. Consider each skill and piece of knowledge you have written above. Use your Mindful Gauge to assess which you can think about sharing while remaining calm. Circle those.

   If you do not currently feel calm about sharing any of these, it may be that you are not ready for that part yet. Nonetheless, you may still be able to consider other parts to this exercise so that you can refer to them when you feel ready to do so. Use the review section in the Ready or Not exercise to reassess your readiness in the future.

4. Consider who might benefit from knowing this information or skill. There are some suggestions in the table below. When you think of more, add them in the spaces. Circle any who you think would benefit from the skill or knowledge you circled above.

   Like Affi, you might want to share your skills spontaneously, when they arise in your life. It might be with a friend, neighbor, family member. Alternatively or in addition, you might want to consider organizing a more formal skill-share privately, at a local charity, or in a blog. If the idea of a blog is appealing, one place to start is Tumblr.com. Babette has found lots of blogs there written by trauma survivors sharing skills that she has passed on to clients and also to participants in her professional trainings. Among others, there are blogs for helping with all sorts of trauma symptoms, including flashbacks, anxiety, self-harm, and such, all written by individuals who have or still suffer from those symptoms and have, nonetheless, discovered skills they have found helpful and wanted to pass on to others.

A specific friend:	A specific family member:	Someone else you know:
A group you are part of, e.g., a theater group or women's circle:	A local charity:	

5. Consider what format you feel comfortable sharing them in. You might want to plan sharing the skills. Consider the suggestions below and circle any that sound good for you.

Writing a blog	Making a zine or booklet	Sharing skills spontaneously with specific people you feel comfortable with
Sharing skills in a social media or support group	Teaching an exercise class	Sharing a walking/cycling/running route

EXTRA GUIDANCE: Sharing skills with others in support groups can definitely be very useful to all concerned.

But a word of caution: Many trauma therapy groups and trauma support groups are structured around the sharing of personal trauma stories, often in great detail. This is not a practice that we condone, because for both the teller and the listeners it can be very triggering. It is for that reason that we suggest that you avoid groups with such a philosophy and practice. Before joining a therapy or support group make sure to talk with the leader about how the group is conducted and what is expected from participants. Then use your Mindful Gauge to determine whether that is something good for you at that point in time.

READY OR NOT?

A variety of factors may affect the way you make lemonade. If you are at a point in your recovery where you are having difficulties with day-to-day tasks, your choice is likely to be different from when you feel in control of your PTSD symptoms.

Affi felt isolated since her trauma and felt overwhelmed whenever she could hear traffic. At home she experienced flashbacks and panic, but she used strategies and tools that she had learned to quickly gain control, feel grounded in the present, and distinguish the traffic sounds she was hearing now from the ones she remembered from the accident. She was able to look after herself and managed to keep to a routine, including getting out of bed at a regular time and doing strengthening exercises each morning. However, she felt too afraid to leave her home. She missed visiting her friends and even missed simple friendly connections such as from another's smile at the store or a hello from her neighbor.

The idea of making lemonade interested her but she was not sure whether she was ready. She saw that helping others would give her a sense of purpose and connection but felt overwhelmed when she thought about going out to do it. She was also concerned about doing anything that might add to her feelings of exhaustion, and worried about letting people down if she felt unable to carry out a commitment on the day.

Affi decided that although she was not sure whether she was ready yet, she could explore some options without pressure, using her Mindful Gauge as her guide. Affi made a list of helping activities that interested her. She was keen to be involved in advocacy to reduce road accidents similar to the one she had experienced. However, she found that focusing on things that reminded her of the accident made her symptoms worse. Though disappointed about her current limitations, she was pleased to have identified a future calling. She decided to check in with herself at regular intervals to see if she felt ready to take on some of that advocacy work, perhaps at first from home.

In addition, Affi identified that there were some other things she could do now from home. Though Affi was not currently working, her career as a chef was a fantastic skill. Using her Mindful Gauge, she decided that she would bake treats for others. She baked bread, cookies, and cakes for her friends and family and then sent them using a delivery service that collected the parcels from her home. Once she felt more confident, she contacted a local charity that provided meals to those in need and baked and sent cookies to them also. She made sure to keep a relaxed pace and checked her Mindful Gauge often so that she did not overload herself.

Knowing what you are ready for can seem tricky, but the Mindful Gauge (Key 1) is likely to be useful.

METHOD

Using the prompts in the boxes below, consider your current capabilities. Apply your Mindful Gauge to assess which, if any, are right for you to share at the moment. Make sure to start small, and stop while you still have energy to do more; that is definitely preferable to becoming overwhelmed by taking on too much too soon.

1. Reflect on the helping activities you would like to do that you listed in the previous exercises. Use your Mindful Gauge to choose one that seems most compatible with your current capabilities, goals, and needs.
2. Make a list of organizations, groups, and charities that have volunteering opportunities in the areas you would like. An internet search might be a good place to start. Your local store or community notice boards might also offer useful information.
3. As in the buddy exercise in Key 7, it might be good to choose a friend whom you can share with and who will encourage you. It can be a fine line between not being ready for something and simply needing a little encouragement if you are nervous. You might even ask a friend to come along with you. Making lemonade is good for everyone, not just those that have experienced trauma. If you know someone who already helps others in a way that you would like to do, you might ask if they could bring you into their project.

4. Write any activities that you would like to do in the future but are not currently ready for. Make a date to review your capabilities. Maybe in a week, several weeks, or several months, reassess whether you are more able to do it. You can use the next exercise, Small Steps to Lemonade, to identify something that is manageable right now and that will lead to that activity in the future.

How regularly could you help without feeling exhausted or overwhelmed?
e.g., once a week/month

What type of setting or location would you feel most calm helping?
e.g., outdoors, at home, in a busy place, a quiet indoor space

What duration could you help for without feeling exhausted or overwhelmed?
e.g., 15 minutes or less, an hour, 3 hours, a full day

Who do you know that might be a helping buddy to give you encouragement or go along with you?

From your research, what groups, organizations, and charities have volunteering opportunities in the areas that you would enjoy?

Helping activities I am interested in but do not feel ready for at the moment:	Review date

SMALL STEPS TO LEMONADE

You may have identified a helping activity that you would love to do but do not feel ready for yet. Or it might be such a big task that it feels daunting. You may have chosen the activity and feel confident about getting started. Whichever is applicable to you, figuring out small steps toward the goal, as we did in Key 6, is likely to be useful.

When Vanessa decided to open a community bike project she felt excited but also overwhelmed. To make her goal manageable, she split the task into smaller and smaller, then tinier and tinier, steps so that it felt achievable one step at a time. You might be surprised to know that her first step was simply inviting a trusted friend out on a bike ride with her and nothing more.

Affi was keen to get started with sending out the baked goods but the task as a whole felt too huge. Writing a list of steps helped her to stay calm and motivated without feeling it was too much. She worked backward:

6. Organize collection by a courier.
5. Put them in a box and write the addresses.
4. Make and bake them.
3. Order mailing boxes for the cakes and cookies.
2. Order the ingredients to be delivered to her home.
1. Find a good recipe for the particular item.

When she looked at her steps she realized that Step 6 actually needed to be Step 1. She felt much calmer making her baked goods when she already knew there was a system in place for getting them sent. She also divided Step 4 into smaller steps. Sometimes she would measure ingredients on one day and wait to combine them the next day, or split the tasks between morning and afternoon, all so she would not be doing too much at once. She also discovered cookie-dough recipes that could be frozen before baking so that she could make a big batch and put half in the freezer for baking at a later time.

METHOD

1. Write your desired helping activity at the top of the arrow. No matter how big or small your helping activity, break it into steps so small that you could start one of them today.
2. Working backward, list the various steps.
3. Review your steps and adjust the order, or add in even smaller steps, until you feel calm with the procedure.

_____

_____

_____

_____

_____

_____

_____

_____

ASSESS YOUR CURRENT
COMMITMENT CAPABILITIES

In addition to time and location considerations, there may be other limits you wish to put in place to help you feel calm when making lemonade. These may be temporary limitations while you are starting out, and regularly reviewing and adapting them to suit you is likely to be beneficial.

Affi was asked by her brother to bake a birthday cake for his friend. Checking in with her Mindful Gauge she noticed that she felt panicked about whether she would feel well enough on the day it was needed. She declined, but gave the details of a great bakery she knew. At that time, she wanted to keep her baking spontaneous so that she did not feel pressure.

Affi reviewed her commitment limits each week and after 6 weeks decided that she would start to offer one special order from a friend or family member per month, if they gave her at least 2 weeks' notice. This gave her plenty of time to prepare, and gave her a few days' leeway in case she was not up to it on one of the days. Applying the principles of Key 6 alongside her Mindful Gauge (Key 1) enabled her to go at a pace that was right for her. Thinking through and being clear about her current capabilities, and holding those boundaries, was essential. Saying no to her brother had been difficult. She did not want to let him down, but she knew that it was essential to her recovery. Keeping your own needs in mind and pacing yourself are vital.

When Vanessa started sharing her bicycle-related skills, she reviewed her list of triggers (Key 4) so that she was more able to preempt flashbacks and overwhelm. These informed another list of her current limits. Initially she chose to cycle only with women, or with men whom she already knew well. If she was repairing a bike from home, she gave her address only to trusted friends. One of her friends agreed to pick up and drop off bikes for other people. When she started running workshops elsewhere, she planned them during the day and in public places.

These boundaries helped her to feel safe, and regularly reviewing what felt okay helped her to continually adapt to meet her needs. It also meant that she avoided feeling resentful, which could sometimes happen if she did not hold her boundaries. If something did not feel right or did not work, she adapted it.

Sometimes, you may be asked to do something that is on your list of limitations. For example, you may be asked to stay later than you planned at a project or, like Affi, asked for something you are not yet ready to do. Having a few stock phrases practiced and ready can help you to hold those limits and calmly say no.

1. Use your Mindful Gauge and list of triggers from Key 4 to help you make a list of limitations and considerations you would like to respect at the moment.

2. How often will you review these?

Weekly on a _____ day	Monthly, on the _____ of the month	Other:

3. Write some stock phrases to help you to say no to requests that you do not want to do at the moment. We have made some suggestions; add your own or rewrite the ones below in your own words.

I am unable to do that today.

I am unable to commit to that at the moment, but I know a great . . . (bakery/bike shop, etc.)
Today I can help for _____ minutes/hours

I am feeling tired, I am leaving early today.

At the moment I am offering this to _____ (e.g., people I know/small groups)

I am currently limiting my hours to _____ (e.g., daytime/morning)

....
....
....
....
....
....
....

4. Practice saying them out loud so that you feel prepared to hold your boundaries if you need to. Remember, it is likely that the person is asking you because they value your help and do not necessarily know your limits. Letting them know can help create a better relationship.

A TRIAL RUN

By now you may have a good idea of what you would like to do, where, with whom, and how often. You may have done some research and found an organization or group to join to help with or have a list of things to do on your own.

A useful thing for many people is to imagine doing the new activity before actually doing it, to double-check whether it is right for them so that they can tweak it before they do it for the first time. Of course, you cannot account for all possibilities in your imagination, but you will likely be able to head off some potential difficulties and add some missed benefits. In sports, imaginal practice is often used as a part of perfecting skills, including in ice-skating and tennis. Downhill mountain-bike racers visualize doing their race run from the comfort of their hotel room. They visualize doing the same race run using multiple different lines down the track and then pick the line they feel most comfortable imagining. Many are able to visualize doing a run to within a couple of seconds of how long it actually takes them once they ride it in real life.

John considered his abilities and current time commitments and decided to offer to purchase and deliver groceries for his neighbor, who he had seen struggling in the past. John was strong and enjoyed physical activities, and he had a car and enjoyed getting out of the house for short trips. He decided he would offer to make the trip only during the day and to the particular store that he knew was quiet during the daytime. He had identified a neighbor he knew well and so did not feel too nervous about approaching.

John was pretty sure he had considered all of the important aspects of his activity and was setting himself up to succeed in a task that was small enough for him at the moment and with someone he trusted. However, he was still a little nervous.

Before doing it for real he imagined the whole scenario: asking the neighbor if she needed help, letting the neighbor know exactly what the terms of the offer were, and so on. He used his Mindful Gauge to check whether it felt okay if the neighbor agreed, or said no. He imagined doing the grocery shopping: driving to the store, collecting the items on the list, driving back, handing the bags to his neighbor, and getting the reimbursement for the purchase. Imagining the task, he felt a little less nervous and a sense of the warm glow he hoped to feel from actually helping.

Then he did a trial run to the shop. He drove from his home, to the store, bought some items, and then drove back, using his Mindful Gauge throughout. He realized that the route he had planned to take was busier than he had expected. On a second trial run he adjusted the route and felt much calmer. Then he felt confident that it was something he was ready for.

Imagining and doing a trial run might help give you confidence before starting the task you have planned.

METHOD

1. List the steps that you will take during your task. This is similar to the task in Key 6. Splitting down the tasks may also make them feel more achievable.
2. As John did, imagine doing each one, checking in with your Mindful Gauge to assess your response and whether anything needs tweaking.
3. If it is appropriate to your helping task, do a trial run, as when John drove the route to the store. Affi made cakes for herself the first time to assess how she felt after a morning of baking (and then had the benefit of being able to enjoy the cake herself). Use your Mindful Gauge to assess whether you need to make any changes.

Write the steps of your helping task in the boxes below. If you need additional boxes, draw them in.

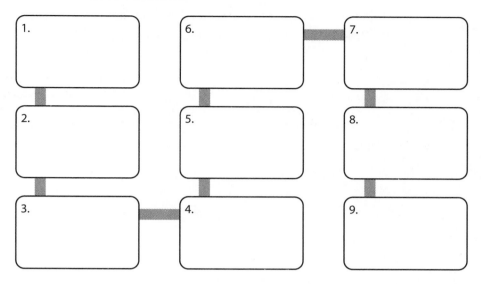

1.

2.

3.

4.

5.

6.

7.

8.

9.

Using your Mindful Gauge, assess whether you need to make any adjustments to the task and note them here:

Imagine doing the task with your adjustments. Does it feel better, worse, or the same?

Do a trial run of the helping task. Note any adjustments that would help you feel better.

Key Review

Did you remember to use your Mindful Gauge to evaluate the exercises in this chapter? If not, was that by choice or because you forgot?

	Did this exercise help, or make you feel worse?	If it helped, what reaction did you have that told you it helped? (For example, felt calmer or stronger or more present.)
What I Value Now		
Pay It Forward		
How to Help		
Kintsugi		
Ready or Not?		
Small Steps to Lemonade		
Assess Your Current Commitment Capabilities		
A Trial Run		

If you forgot, consider whether you want to go back and do that.
Once you have completed an exercise you may wish to jot down your response and its effectiveness for you in the table.

If it helped, could it be adapted to help more? How?	If it helped, when do you plan to use it?	If it did not help, could you change or adapt it to better suit you? How?

References

We have included the details here of the references in the Keys for your information. We do not want to overload you with additional things to read, but we do know that for some of you these may be of interest.

KEY 1

Damasio, A. (1994). *Descartes' error: Emotion, reason, and the human brain*. Avon Books.

Trousselard, M., Steiler, D., Claverie, D., & Canini, F. (2014). L'histoire de la Mindfulness à l'épreuve des données actuelles de la littérature: Questions en suspens [The history of Mindfulness put to the test of current scientific data: Unresolved questions]. *Encephale*, 40(6), 474–480. Advance online publication. https://doi.org/10.1016/j.encep.2014.08.006

KEY 2

Rothschild, B. (2010). *8 Keys to Safe Trauma Recovery: Take-charge strategies to empower your healing*. W. W. Norton.

Siegel, D. J. (2010). *Mindsight: The new science of personal transformation*. Bantam Books.

KEY 3

Angelou, M. (2011, January 16). Be a rainbow in someone else's cloud. *Oprah's Master Class*, OWN.

Badenoch, B. (2008). *Being a brain-wise therapist: A practical guide to interpersonal neurobiology*. W. W. Norton.

Janet, P. (1973). *L'automatisme psychologique* [Psychological automatism]. Société Pierre Janet. (Original work published 1889)

Rowling, J. K. (2014). *Harry Potter and the deathly hallows*. New York: Bloomsbury Children's Books.

KEY 5

Roberts, D. L., Thronson, F., & Gavin, M. (2017). *Able & equal*. Not So Common Publishing.

KEY 6

Copage, E. V. (1996). *Black pearls: Daily meditations, affirmations, and inspirations for African-Americans*. William Morrow.

KEY 7

Rothschild, B. (2000). *The body remembers: The psychophysiology of trauma and trauma treatment*. W. W. Norton.

KEY 8

Okun, M. A., Yeung, E. W., & Brown, S. (2013). Volunteering by older adults and risk of mortality: A meta-analysis. *Psychology and Aging, 28*(2). https://doi.org/10.1037/a0031519

Sneed, R. S., & Cohen, S. (2013). A prospective study of volunteerism and hypertension risk in older adults. *Psychology and Aging, 28*(2), 578–586.

Schreier, H. M. C., Schonert-Reichl, K. A., & Chen, E. (2013). Effect of volunteering on risk factors for cardiovascular disease in adolescents: A randomized controlled trial. *JAMA Pediatrics, 167*(4), 327–332. https://doi.org/10.1001/jamapediatrics.2013.1100

Wang, Y., Ge, J., Zhang, H., Wang, H., & Xie, X. (2019). Altruistic behaviors relieve physical pain. *Proceedings of the National Academy of Sciences, 117*(2), 950–958. Advance online publication. https://doi.org/10.1073/pnas.1911861117

Index

Note: Italicized page locators refer to figures; tables are noted with a *t*.

Able and Equal (Roberts & Thronson), 176
adversity
    helping others and, 247–48
    overcoming, 246
advocating your pace, 203–5, 208*t*
    examples and replies, writing, 205
    rehearsing your responses, 204
affirmations, 153
Altruistic behaviors relieve physical pain
        (Wang et al.), 291
amygdala, 41, 138, 139, 150
    Fast Response and, 142
    Slow Response and, 143
    survival and, 139, 140
Anchors to Now list, examples, 115
Angelou, M., 38, 147, 290
animals, shame and, 158
anxiety, xv
arms
    left, muscle toning and, 237–38
    right, muscle toning and, 238
autonomic nervous system responses, 140–
        41, 180*t*
autopilot, mindfulness *vs.*, 2
avoidance, as a friend, 185–88

Badenoch, B., 54, 290
balance, finding stability through, 92–93, 93,
        102*t*

balance, moving with, 239–41, 244*t*
    book and ball balance, 241
    building-blocks balance, 240–41, 241*t*
    finding your center, 239–40
Bareilles, S., 167
Bear, V., 49, 62, 85, 89, 94, 189, 199, 203,
        211, 225, 246, 250, 264, 279, 281
Be a rainbow in someone else's cloud
        (Angelou), 290
Being a brain-wise therapist (Badenoch), 290
being here, now kit, 117, *118*, 134*t*
belly breathing, lengthening your exhalation
        and, 99
bicycling, 212, 229*t*
bike project, community, 263–64, 279, 281
Black Pearls (Copage), 184
blogs, by trauma survivors sharing skills,
        272–73
boat, miniature, 49
Bodynamic Institute (Copenhagen,
        Denmark), 65, 237
Body Remembers, The (Rothschild), 237, 291
body sensations
    checking in with, 3–4, 28*t*
    flashbacks and, 104, 105
    safe-place memory and, 76
    shame and, 161, *161*
    see also boundaries; senses; triggers
book and ball balance, 241

"Born to Fight" (Chapman), 166
boundaries
    advocating your pace and, 203
    commitment limits and, 281–82, 284
    protective, describing, 119–20, 134t
    protective, drawing, 121, *121*, 134t
    sharing your shame to connect/reconnect
        with others and, 174
    see also body sensations; commitment
        limits, assessing; containment
brain
    "flipped lid" and, 41, *42*
    hand model of, 41, *41*
    three main parts of, 41, *41*
brain stem, 41, *41*, 42
"Brave" (Bareilles), 167
breathing
    noticing your stable breath, 96–97, 102t
    using your breath to stabilize, 98–99, 102t
building-blocks balance, 240–41, 241t
bullying, shamelessness and, 158

caffeine, 239
calm, making a date with, 85–86, *86*, 102t
celebrating your survival, 49–51, 52t
chairs, choosing the right one, 89–91, *90*,
    102t
Chapman, T., 166
checking in, 3–4, 28t
Cher, 166
Christianity, mindfulness and roots in, 1
clay, putting shame back where it belongs
    and, 165, 166
Cohen, S., 291
collage
    putting shame back where it belongs and,
        165
    Soul Collage, 45
comfort zone, routines and rituals and, 70.
    see also boundaries
commitment limits, assessing, 281–84, 288t
    stock phrases to use, 283

triggers and, 281
    see also boundaries
community gardens, 219
community trauma, helping others and,
    247–48
compassion
    being accountable and compassionate
        with yourself, 176–79, 182t
    connecting with, 147
    finding for your younger self, 146
    forgive-your-limitations letter and, 154
    see also helping others; kindness; make
        lemonade (key 8)
containment, muscle toning and, 236, 237.
    see also boundaries
Copage, E. V., 184
cortex, 41, *41*
    "flipped lid" and, 42
    Slow Response and, 143
Couch to 5K, 184–85
COVID-19 pandemic, helping others
    during, 247–48, 263
creative, calming patterns, 94, *94–95*, 95, 102t
cuboids, two-object balance and, 93

Damasio, A., 5, 290
dancing, 229t
    as low-impact exercise, 212
    putting shame back where it belongs and,
        167
decision-making
    mindful approach to, 1
    somatic markers and, 5
Descartes' error (Damasio), 290
Destiny's Child, 166
dissociation, 140
"Don't Stop" (Fleetwood Mac), 166
dopamine
    exercise and increase in, 210
    helping others and release of, 247
drawing and painting, putting shame back
    where it belongs and, 165

Effect of volunteering on risk factors for cardiovascular disease in adolescents (Schreier et al.), 291

8 Keys to Safe Trauma Recovery (Rothschild), xvi, 49, 203, 290

emotions, safe-place memory and, 77

empowering objects, as "now objects," 113, 132*t*

endorphins, exercise and increase in, 210

epilogue, beginning with (key 2), xviii, 16*t*, 32–53

  celebrate and honor your survival, 49–51, 52*t*

  current resources, 36–37, 52*t*

  identify your rainbows, and bring them with you, 38–40, 39, 52*t*

  I survived!, 47–48, 52*t*

  timeline, 41–43, 44, 52*t*

  your epilogue, 45–46, 52*t*

epilogue, definition of, 32

Esso, S., 167

exercise

  benefits of, 210

  low-impact, 212

  tracking with charts or graphs, 223, 224*t*

  see also get moving (key 7)

exercise buddy, finding, 222, 222*t*, 242*t*

exhalation, lengthening, 96, 98

external stimuli, flashbacks and, 105, 107, 108, 132*t*

false memories, 57

Fast Response, amygdala and, 142

fatigue

  exercise and, 234

  trauma survivors and, 211–12

"Feeling Good" (Simone), 167

finding your center, 239–40

fire ritual, 49

flashbacks, xv, 75, 168, 203, 268, 275, 281

  disturbing features of, 104

  feelings of loss of control and, 137

  managing, splitting one goal into steps, 193–94

  see also triggers

flashbacks, stopping (key 4), xix, 16*t*, 104–35

  being here, now kit, 117, *118*, 134*t*

  draw your protective boundary, 121, *121*, 134*t*

  empower objects, 113, 132*t*

  flashback triggers and resources, 122–25, 134*t*

  individualized procedure, example of, 130

  internal and external, 107–8, *108*, 132*t*

  making a plan for preempting, 127, 134*t*

  mantra: that was a memory, 111, 132*t*

  noticing patterns, 126, 134*t*

  other anchors to now, 114, 132*t*

  present-day fact sheet, 115–16, 132*t*

  protective boundaries, 119–20, 134*t*

  self-talk: that was a memory, 109–10, 132*t*

  taking control of your flashback, 128–31, 134*t*

  what can help, 105–6

flee, fight, or freeze responses, 41, 138, 140, 141, 143

Fleetwood Mac, 166

focus

  attention and, increasing, 87–88, 88, 102*t*

  building-blocks balance and, 240–41, 241*t*

forgiveness

  choices related to, 136

  of others, 136

  of your limitations, 136–39

  see also reconcile forgiveness and shame (key 5); self-forgiveness

forgive-your-limitations letter, 154–55, 182*t*

forgive-your-limitations mantra, 153, 180*t*

Frank, A., 246

freeze response, movement as antidote to, 210

frontal cortex, 41, *41*

gardening, 219, 220
Gavin, M., 187
Gaynor, G., 166, 167
get moving (key 7), xix, 17t, 210–45
  breaking freeze response with movement, 210
  connecting with your strength, 234–35, 244t
  find an exercise buddy, 222, 242t
  find your activity, 214–15, 215, 242t
  habit-making movement, 225–26, 244t
  movement in nature, 219–20, 220, 242t
  moving with balance, 239–41, 244t
  muscle toning, 236–38, 244t
  with others or alone?, 212
  posture, 231–33, 244t
  set up record keeping, 223–24, 224t, 242t
  small steps and alternatives, 216–18, 218, 242t
  time-saving movement habits, 227–30, 228t, 229, 229t, 244t
goals
  advocating your pace relative to, 203–5, 208t
  going slow with, 197–98, 198, 206t
  recovery, 192, 206t
  small, achievable steps to, 185
  splitting into manageable steps, 196, 206t
  splitting one goal into steps, 193–94, 195, 206t
  supported steps and, 201–2, 208t
  taking alternative steps to, 199–200, 200, 206t
going numb, 140
Goldilocks, 8, 10, 65
  choosing the right chair, 89–91, 90, 102t
  choosing the right therapist for you, 65
  finding your center and, 240
  helping others and, 264
  making a date with calm, 85
golf, 212

Grey's Anatomy, 231
grounding, 70
guilt, 137, 138, 142, 158, 178

habit-making movement, 225–26, 244t
Hand model of the brain, 41, 41
Harry Potter and the Deathly Hallows (Rowling), 291
Harry Potter series, epilogue in, 32
health, helping others and, 247
helping others
  assessing your current capabilities for, 276–78
  benefits of, 247
  choosing a buddy for, 276
  choosing type of activity for, 265t–267t
  see also kindness
hiking, 212
hippocampus, 41, 42
Hippocrates, 210
History of Mindfulness, The (Trousselard et al.), 290
hope, helping others and, 248
houseplants, 219, 220
Houston, W., 166
Hubbard, E., 246

"I Am What I Am" (Gaynor), 166
images, safe-place memory and, 77
imaginal practice, 285
"I'm Coming Out" (Ross), 166
"I'm Still Standing" (Elton John), 166
inhalation, 96, 98
internal sensations, flashbacks and, 104, 105, 107–8, 108, 132t
interpersonal resources, 37, 38, 69
intrusive memories, self-talk and, 109
in vivo exposure, 33–34
Islam, mindfulness and roots in, 1
isolation
  shame and, 168, 169
  trauma and, 248, 275
"I Will Survive" (Gaynor), 167

Janet, P., 55, 57, 291
John, E., 166
Judaism, mindfulness and roots in, 1
jumping rope, 229t

kindness, simple acts of, 248, 260. *see also* compassion; helping others; make lemonade (key 8)
kintsugi, 268–70, 270, 272, 272–73, 288t
  origin of, 268
  trauma recovery and art of, 268
  videos on art of, 269

L'automatisme psychologique (Janet), 291
legs, muscle toning and side of, 237
limbic system, 41, *41*, 42, 138
limitations, forgiving, 137–39
linking activities together, strengthening habits through, 225, 227, 228, 229, 229
loneliness, trauma and, 248. *see also* isolation

make lemonade (key 8), xix, 17t, 246–89
  assess your current commitment capabilities, 281–84, 288t
  how to help, 263–64, 265t–267t, 288t
  kintsugi, 268–70, 270, 272, 272–73, 273t, 288t
  pay it forward, 260–62, 262, 288t
  ready or not?, 275–78, 288t
  small steps to lemonade, 279–80, 288t
  story behind name for, 246
  a trial run, 285–87, 287, 288t
  what I value now, 250–59, 288t
mandalas
  drawing, 94, 94–95, 95
  nature or object, 95
  religious practices and, 94
mantra, definition of, 153
massage, 236
"Mean" (Swift), 166
meditation, 2, 236

meeting your own needs, giving yourself permission, 211
memory(ies)
  false, 57
  intrusive, self-talk and, 109
  safe-place, 75–78, 76, 100t
  of trauma, complete or partial loss of, 56
  see also flashbacks, stopping (key 4); remembering is not required (key 3)
mental health, helping others and, 247
Me Too movement, 168
Mindful Gauge, 3, 8–16, 16t, 28t, 35, 43, 52, 100, 106, 127, 129
  balancing objects and, 92
  breathing pattern and, 98
  celebrating your survival and, 50
  choosing the right chair and, 89, 90
  commitment limits and, 281, 282
  current resources and, 36
  drawing your protective boundaries and, 121
  exercise and, 212, 213, 214, 225–26
  Goldilocks, as gauge role model, 8, 10, 65
  helping others and, 249, 275, 276
  making a date with calm and, 85
  making best use of, 8–9
  mantras and, 153
  method for, 10–11, 13–14
  moving with balance and, 239
  muscle tone assessment and, 237
  options, 12t
  paying it forward and, 262
  plotting your course with, 15–16, 16t, 28t
  putting shame back where it belongs and, 164
  rainbow memories and, 40
  reconciling forgiveness and shame and, 139
  safe-place memory and, 78
  sharing in support groups and, 274
  sharing your recovery skills and, 272
  sharing your shame to connect/reconnect with others and, 169, 170, 171, 172, 175
stabilization breaks and, 74

Mindful Gauge (*continued*)
  taking steps to achieve your goals and, 186, 188, 198, 200, 201, 202, 204
  trial runs and, 285, 286, 287
  using with phased trauma treatment approach, 58, 63, 65, 66
  values exercise and, 252
mindfulness
  autopilot *vs.*, 2
  decision-making and, 1
  definition of, 2
  gaining mastery over flashbacks and, 107
  history behind, 1
mindfulness, plotting your course with (key 1), xviii, 1–31
  being here, now, with sight, 25, 30*t*
  being here, now, with smell, 23–24, 30*t*
  being here, now, with sound, 26, 30*t*
  being here, now, with taste, 22, 30*t*
  being here, now, with touch, 27, 30*t*
  checking in, 3–4, 28*t*
  key review, 28*t*–31*t*
  Mindful Gauge, 8–14, 28*t*
  mindful walking, 18–20, 28*t*
  somatic markers, 5–7, 28*t*
  using your Mindful Gauge, 15–16, 16*t*, 28*t*
mindful walking, 18–20, 28*t*
Mindsight (Siegel), 290
mini-movement breaks, 227
mood, posture and, 231
Mothers Against Drunk Driving, 248
motivation, finding your exercise activity and, 214
movement. *see* get moving (key 7)
muscle tensioning, 229*t*
muscle toning, 236–38, 244*t*

natural disasters, helping others and, 247
nature
  movement in, 219–20, 220, 242*t*
  overcoming adversity in, 246
nightmares, 113

"No Scrubs" (TLC), 167
"now objects," empowering objects as, 113, 132*t*
"Numb" (Esso), 167
nutrition, 212

objects, empowering as "now objects," 113, 132*t*
Okun, M. A., 291
one-object balance, 93, 93
oxytocin, helping others and release of, 247

painting. *see* drawing and painting
panic attacks, xv, 21, 113, 203, 234, 268, 275
past, inability to change, 57
past-tense language, self-talk and, 109–10
patterns, noticing, 126, 134*t*
pay it forward, 260–62, 262, 288*t*
Perry, K., 166
phased approach to trauma treatment
  achieving feeling of reliable safety and stabilization (Phase 1), 55, 56, 59, 59, 60, 67
  integration of Phase 1 and 2 in daily life (Phase 3), 55, 56, 57, 58, 59, 59
  Mindful Gauge and, 58, 63, 65, 66
  processing trauma memories (Phase 2), 55, 56, 57, 58, 59, 59, 60, 62, 65, 73
  quality of life and, 56, 57, 62
  what can help, 57–58
  which phase is most useful for right now?, 59–60
physical abuse, stigma attached to, 168
physical assault, shamelessness and, 158
physical resources, 36, 68
plank against a wall, 234, 235
planking, 229*t*
"playing dead," 140
posttraumatic stress disorder (PTSD), xv, 73, 87, 193, 203, 223, 246, 268
  balance, vestibular issues, and, 239
  fatigue and, 211–12

support and healing from, 212
posture, 231–33, 244*t*
practical resources, 36, 68
prefrontal cortex, 42, *42*
present-day fact sheet, 115–16, 132*t*
present-tense verbs, flashbacks and use of, 109–10
pre-steps, on way to achieving goals, 187
proprioception
  balancing objects and, 92
  flashbacks and, 105
Prospective study of volunteerism and hypertension risk in older adults, A (Sneed & Cohen), 291
protective boundaries
  describing, 119–20, 134*t*
  drawing, 121, *121*, 134*t*
psychological resources, 37, 69
purpose, helping others and sense of, 247

rainbows, identifying, and bringing them with you, 38–40, 52*t*
rape, shame and, 163
reconcile forgiveness and shame (key 5), xix, 16*t*, 136–83
  additional limitations, 145, 180*t*
  autonomic nervous system responses, 140–41, 180*t*
  be accountable and compassionate with yourself, 176–79, 182*t*
  forgive your limitations, 136–39
  forgive-your-limitations mantra, 153–55, 182*t*
  how do you know when you feel shame?, 161, *161*, 182*t*
  put shame back where it belongs, 164–67, 182*t*
  relieve your shame, 162–64, 182*t*
  shall, will, can resources, 150–52, 180*t*
  share your shame, 156–57
  share your shame to connect or reconnect with others, 168–75, 182*t*

should have, would have, could have, 146–49, 180*t*
  trauma-response limitations, 142–44, 180*t*
  what is the point of shame?, 158–60, 182*t*
record keeping, exercise and, 223–24, 224*t*, 242*t*
recovery
  goals, 192, 206*t*
  human, animal, and nature support in, 260, 261
  individual journey of, xxi
relaxation, guided, 211
relaxation-induced anxiety, 236
remembering is not required (Key 3), xviii, 16*t*, 54–103, 203
  choosing the right chair, 89–91, 90, 102*t*
  creative, calming patterns, 94, 94–95, 95, 102*t*
  finding stability through balance, 92–93, 93, 102*t*
  increasing focus and attention, 87–88, 88
  make a date with calm, 85–86, 86, 102*t*
  noticing your stable breath, 96–97, 102*t*
  phase most useful to you now, 55–56, 59–60, 100*t*
  pros and cons, 64–67, 100*t*
  routines and rituals, 70–72, 100*t*
  safe-place memory, 75–78, 76, 100*t*
  safety and stability wish list, 68–69, 100*t*
  stabilization breaks, 73–74, 100*t*
  trauma types, 61–64, 100*t*
  using your breath to stabilize, 98–99, 102*t*
  what feeling safe and stable means to you, 79–84, 102*t*
repairing your broken objects, *kintsugi* and, 269–70, 270
resources
  current, 36–37, 52*t*
  physical, 36, 68
  practical, 36, 68
  psychological, 37, 69
  shall, will, can, 150–52

resources (*continued*)
  spiritual, 37, 69
rewards, for exercising, 223, 224
rituals. *see* routines and rituals
"Roar" (Perry), 166
Roberts, D. L., 176
Ross, D., 166
Rothschild, B., xvi, 40, 45, 49, 56, 62, 65, 85,
    87, 184, 203, 223, 237, 263, 269, 290, 291
routines and rituals, 70–72, 100*t*
Rowling, J. K., 291

safe-place memory, 75–78, 76, 100*t*
safety
  healing from trauma and, xvii
  seeking, 107, 130
  see also boundaries; resources
safety and stability
  reliable, achieving feeling of, 55, 56, 59,
    60, 67
  weekly assessment, 81
  what it means to you, 79–84, 102*t*
  wish list, 68–69, 100*t*
Schreier, H. M. C., 291
scripts, sharing your shame and, 173–74
self-blame, 146, 150
self-defense classes, 150
self-esteem, exercising with others and, 222
self-forgiveness, 136–37, 140
  shall, will, can resources and, 150–52
  statements of, 148, 149
self-talk
  forgive-your-limitations mantra, 153
  shall, will, can resources and, 150–52
  that was a memory, 109–10, 132*t*
senses
  flashbacks and, 104
  gaining mastery over flashbacks and, 107,
    108, *108*
  pleasant and grounding things related to, *118*
  protective boundaries and, 119
  rainbow memories and, 39

safe-place memory and, 76
stabilizing your system with, 123
taking control of your flashback with, 129
  see also body sensations; boundaries; sight;
    smell; sound; taste; touch
serotonin
  exercise and increase in, 210
  helping others and release of, 247
Settle, Keala, 166
sexual abuse, stigma attached to, 168
sexual assault, shamelessness and, 158
shall, will, can resources, 150–52, 180*t*
shame, 197
  benefits of, writing about, 159–60
  distinguishing from other emotions, 161,
    161, 182*t*
  healthy, shamelessness *vs.*, 163
  purpose of, 158–59, 182*t*
  relieving, 162, 182*t*
  sharing, 156–57
  sharing to connect/reconnect with others,
    168–75, 182*t*
  writing about feelings of, 171
shame, putting it back where it belongs,
    164–67, 182*t*
  clay, 165, 166
  collage, 165
  dancing, 167
  drawing and painting, 164–65
  singing, 166–67
  writing, 164
shamelessness, 161
  cost of, 158
  healthy shame *vs.*, 163
sharing skills
  blogs and, 272–73
  in support groups, 274
Siegel, D. J., 41, 290
Siffre, L., 167
sight
  balancing objects and, 92
  being here, now, with, 25, 30*t*

gaining mastery over flashbacks and, 107, 108, *108*

pleasant and grounding things related to, *118*

protective boundaries and, 119

safe-place memory and, *76, 77*

Simone, N., 167

singing

    lengthening your exhalation and, 99

    putting shame back where it belongs and, 166–67

sleep, exercise and, 212

Slow Response, amygdala and cortex and, 143

small steps

    helping others and, 249

    to lemonade, 279–80, *288t*

    in paying it forward, 263–64

    reducing everyday tasks to, 189–90, *190–91, 206t*

smell

    being here, now, with, 23–24, *30t*

    gaining mastery over flashbacks and, 107, 108, *108*

    pleasant and grounding things related to, *118*

    protective boundaries and, 119

    safe-place memory and, *76, 77*

    taking control of your flashback with, 129

Sneed, R. S., 291

somatic markers, 5–7, 8, *28t*

somatic marker theory, 5

"(Something inside) So Strong" (Siffre), 167

Soul Collage, 45

sound

    being here, now, with, 26, *30t*

    gaining mastery over flashbacks and, 107, 108, *108*

    pleasant and grounding things related to, *118*

    protective boundaries and, 119

    safe-place memory and, *76, 77*

spiritual resources, 37, 69

sports, imaginal practice in, 285

sports clubs, local, 217

Sports Day, UK, 92

squats, 227, 228, *229t*, 235

stability, finding through balance, 92–93, *93, 102t*

stabilization breaks, 73–74, *100t*

stable breath, noticing, 96–97, *102t*

"Step by Step" (Houston), 166

straw breathing, lengthening your exhalation and, 99

strength, connecting with, 234–35, *244t*

strength training, 210–11, 223, 227, 228, *229t*

stress management, exercise and, 212

"Strong Enough" (Cher), 166

support groups, sharing skills in, cautionary note, 274

survival

    celebrating and honoring, 49–51, *52t*

    recognizing, xvi, xxi, 33, 34, 42, 139

    short statements about, 47–48

"Survivor" (Destiny's Child), 166

Suzy Lamplugh Trust, 248

Swift, T., 166

swimming, 212

take smaller steps for bigger leaps (key 6), xix, *17t*, 34, 184–209

    advocating your pace, 203–5, *208t*

    alternative steps, 199–200, *200, 206t*

    avoidance as a friend, 185–88

    Couch to 5K, 184–85

    go slow, 197–98, *198, 206t*

    manageable steps, 196, *206t*

    recovery goals, 192, *206t*

    reducing to smaller steps, 189–90, *190–91, 206t*

    splitting one goal into steps, 193–95, *206t*

    supported steps, 201–2, *202, 208t*

taste

    being here, now, with, 22, *30t*

taste (*continued*)

    gaining mastery over flashbacks and, 107, 108, *108*

    pleasant and grounding things related to, *118*

    protective boundaries and, 119

    safe-place memory and, 76, 77

technology changes, timeline and, 43, *44*, 45, 47

Thich Nhat Hanh, 210

thighs, muscle toning and, 238

"This Is Me" (Keala Settle), 166

thoughts, safe-place memory and, 77

Thronson, F., 176

timeline, 41–43, 52*t*

    drawing, 43

    example of, *44*

time-saving movement habits, 227–30, 228*t*, 229, 229*t*, 244*t*

tiptoe exercise, 235

TLC, 167

tortoise and hare fable, 187, 197

touch

    being here, now, with, 27, 30*t*

    gaining mastery over flashbacks and, 107, 108, *108*

    pleasant and grounding things related to, *118*

    protective boundaries and, 119

    safe-place memory and, 76

trauma

    helping others and, 247–48

    taking stock of your values after, 250

    types of, 61–63, 100*t*

trauma-response limitations, 142–45, 180*t*

    additional, 145

    Fast Response (amygdala only), 142

    Slow Response (cortex and amygdala), 143

trauma therapy, as relatively new treatment option, 54

trauma treatment, Janet's three-phased approach to, 55, 56, 57, 58, 59, 59, 60, 62

trial runs, 285–87, 288*t*

Mindful Gauge and, 285, 286, 287

    writing helping tasks in boxes, 287

triggers, 105, 107, 168, 176

    assessing commitment limits and, 281

    feelings of loss of control and, 137

    resources and, 122–23, 124*t*–125*t*, 134*t*

    reviewing, commitment limits and, 281

    see also flashbacks; Mindful Gauge

Trousselard, M., 290

Tumblr.com, 272

two-object balance, 93, *93*

values

    currently represented in your life, 257

    gaps in, 258

    most important to you, 255–56

    rating, exercise for, 251–54

    taking stock of, 250–58, 288*t*

vestibular sense, balancing objects and, 92

victims of trauma, 138

visualizing, 285–86. *see also* sight

volunteering, 263, 276

Volunteering by older adults and risk of mortality (Okun et al.), 291

vowel sounds, lengthening your exhalation and, 99

wabi sabi, 268

walking, 212, 216, 223, 225, 229*t*, 231–32

    journal, 20

    mindful, 18–20, 28*t*

Wang, Y., 291

Washington, B. T., 246

water ritual, 49

writing

    putting shame back where it belongs through, 164

    your epilogue, 45–46, 52*t*

Yellowstone National Park, gray wolves reintroduced into, 250

yoga, 212, 216, 225, 226, 236

About the Authors

Babette Rothschild, MSW, has been a practitioner since 1976 and a teacher and trainer since 1992. She is the author of six books (translated into more than a dozen languages including Danish, German, French, Spanish, and Japanese), all published by W. W. Norton: *Revolutionizing Trauma Treatment* (2017, 2021); her classic bestseller, *The Body Remembers* (2000); *The Body Remembers CASEBOOK* (2003); *Help for the Helper* (2022, 2005); *8 Keys to Safe Trauma Recovery* (2010); and *Trauma Essentials* (2010). She is the series editor of Norton's 8 Keys to Mental Health series. After living and working for nine years in Copenhagen, Denmark, she returned to her native Los Angeles. There, she is writing her next books while she continues to lecture, train, and supervise professional psychotherapists worldwide. For more information, visit her website: www.trauma.cc

Vanessa Bear is a psychotherapeutic counselor with experience of working with children, adolescents, and adults in the National Health Service, schools, charities, and in private practice in the UK. She is a registered member of the BACP professional body and works to their high ethical standards. Much of Vanessa's work is with people who have experienced, and are recovering from, trauma, including domestic abuse and sexual assault.

Vanessa believes in a highly individualized approach and draws on her training and qualifications in psychotherapeutic counseling; somatic trauma therapy; coaching; nature connection; creativity; dance and movement; forest school; yoga and mindfulness; traditional crafts; and mountain walking.

Prior to working as a counselor, Vanessa has worked as a primary school teacher, forest school leader, youth worker, yoga teacher, mountain guide, bicycle mechanic, and has run a bicycle community project.

Vanessa lives in the Lake District, UK with her partner, two dogs, and horse, where she takes nourishment and inspiration from nature.